Naturally Healthy First Foods

for Baby

The Best Nutrition for the First Year and Beyond

• Jacqueline Rubin •

SOURCEBOOKS, INC.
NAPERVILLE, ILLINOIS

Published by Sourcebooks, Inc.
P.O. Box 4410, Naperville, Illinois 60567-4410
(630) 961-3900
Fax: (630) 961-2168
www.sourcebooks.com

Library of Congress Cataloging-in-Publication Data

Rubin, Jacqueline.
  Naturally healthy first foods for baby : the best nutrition for the first year and beyond / Jacqueline Rubin.
    p. cm.
  Includes index.
  1. Infants--Nutrition. 2. Cookery (Baby foods) 3. Cookery (Natural foods) I. Title.

RJ216.R83 2008
649'.3--dc22
                            2007044206

Printed and bound in the United States of America
VP 10 9 8 7 6 5 4 3 2

Dedication

To my children Seth and Breana, whose love and whose good taste in food inspired this book.

Contents

Acknowledgments

I would like to express my sincere gratitude to everyone who helped make this book a reality by providing insight and guidance, and who were there when needed. First and foremost I give thanks to my editors at Sourcebooks for their guidance and patience: Bethany Brown, Shana Drehs, Ewurama Ewusi-Mensah, Sara Appino, and Dojna Shearer.

To my children Seth and Breana, my original taste-testers, for telling me to hurry up and finish this book so I could spend more time with them.

To my husband Lawrence, my cooking partner, who realized the benefits of, and openly embraced, a whole-foods diet for Seth and Breana and encouraged me to undertake this project.

To my father-in-law Sam Rubin for his child-entertaining and chauffeuring duties.

And to my brothers Arlan and Richard, who always challenged me to learn more.

This book owes much to those in the medical profession who took time out from their busy schedules to review sections of the manuscript relating to food introduction and allergies, or to simply discuss topics with me: Dr. Mickey Lester, Dr. Martin Kosoy, Dr. Alan Berzen, Dr. Gary Rubin, Dr. Christopher Hassell.

Sincere thanks to the expert advice from Paul Pitchford from the Heartwood Institute in California, Zara Fischer-Harrison and Marie Larsson at Toronto Sprouts, and Sproutman Steve Meyerowitz.

Thank you to my extended support group: Dr. Bill Fisher and his sense of humor that helped keep me organized and on schedule, and kept my computers happily humming. For keeping me centered and balanced throughout the writing process, thanks to my wonderful yoga instructors, Axel Molema, Diane Bruni, Ron Reid, Xenia Splawinski, and Fern Morrison (no small task, which is why there are five of them), the Andrea Olivera Centre for Ayurveda, and Elizabeth Abraham of the Vision Education Centre.

To Dr. Sam Klarreich for believing in this project and help making it a reality.

To my many friends and neighbors who were there when needed: Howard Brown, who was a great sounding board; Myrna Berlin; Diane Silver-Hassell; Charlene Day; Mikki Fox; Eleanore Carson, Bev Michaels; Sandra Temes, a great chef and cookbook author; and my swimming and yoga buddies.

Thanks to all the moms and babies who eagerly taste-tested my recipes and offered valuable suggestions for this book.

Heartfelt thanks to my mother, who took the time to feed me whole natural foods as a child, and who inspired me to write this book.

Introduction

While eating your breakfast this morning with your baby in your lap, you may have realized that her two tiny hands were reaching for your food. Although it might seem like just yesterday that you brought your little bundle of joy home, she is now six months old, and she wants to have what you're eating. Now is the time to toss the takeout menus that you have been relying on for the last few months and get reacquainted with your kitchen.

Naturally Healthy First Foods for Baby is a guidebook with recipes, presented in a simple, informative format that will show you how to prepare wholesome, homemade baby foods with room for your intuition, your inventiveness, and your baby's tastes. This book is intended for all parents and caregivers who want to give their babies the best possible start in life. By following specific feeding steps when your baby starts solid foods, you can reduce the potential risk of allergies and future digestive, immune, and nervous system disorders, and you can promote optimal brain development.

As soon as I found out about my first pregnancy, I began to read everything on the topic of baby nutrition, as I was a nutritionist. I found much controversy in the search for the "best" diet, and I began developing a homemade food program that was nutritious, tasty, and simple to prepare, and used organic, whole ingredients and mother's intuition. Most societies do not have books on this subject: they rely instead on cultural and familial sources for advice on how and what to feed the next generation.

In North America, book upon book tries to establish the best baby food diet. Advice for new parents is plentiful and often confusing, leaving parents to wonder whether or not what they are doing is right. What is sometimes lost is that every baby is unique, and so there is no absolute right or wrong that applies to all babies. This book will take you on a wonderful journey toward creating healthy independent eaters. I will show you how to feel confident about your choices, and how to learn to listen to your intuition as you nurture your child.

Environmental factors have a role to play in childhood ailments. A diet at the weaning stage made up of whole, natural, organic foods, largely plant based, with moderate amounts of animal products if desired, will not overload your children with pesticides, antibiotics, or hormones from animals. The key is to not be too restrictive or too lax in the foods you introduce. This book contains safe, tested, physician-approved recommendations for feeding your baby solid foods. It will make your decisions easy rather than overwhelming.

The reason for my reliance on whole foods is twofold. First, as a mother and a nutritionist, I firmly believe that whole foods are best for Baby. Second, all cultures at one time or another relied solely on local whole foods for their entire diet from birth through adulthood. *Naturally Healthy First Foods for Baby* is based on principles that have been used successfully for countless generations. As modern life becomes more unbalanced, and as we take on more and more responsibilities, many of us have turned to and embraced teachings of Asian cultures, such as yoga, Ayurveda (India), macrobiotics (Japan), and *chi kung* (China). A common thread within these cultures is that good digestion is the key to radiant health. It is not only the wealthy Hollywood stars who have embraced the natural foods movement; it may be as close as your next-door neighbor, or even you!

Without question, there are quicker, easier routes to feeding your baby than the one outlined here. However, with minimal extra time and effort you can reap significant benefits: strong, healthy children with lean bodies and good eating habits, which will stay with them for a lifetime.

I think your children are worth it! Don't you?

Jacqueline Rubin
June, 2007

NOTE: The terms *he* and *she* are used interchangeably throughout the book to represent no child in particular.

chapter 1

The Journey Begins in You

"As she is the nourisher, she should be nourished.
The woman carries the Spirit as an embryo."

—Aitareya Upanishad

Part 1: Nutrition during Pregnancy

The miracle of life begins in you. As you embark on the wonderful journey of pregnancy, nourish yourself well, because your baby grows out of your love, your joy, and how you take care of yourself. Nurturing yourself with healthy, whole foods ensures that your unborn baby, who shares the food you eat, gets the best possible beginning. A good diet during pregnancy will help your baby's brain and body grow in the womb, and you can feel confident that she will continue to thrive on your high-quality breast milk after birth.

Eating well also ensures that *you* remain strong throughout pregnancy. When your body is well nourished, you will feel energetic and excited, instead of depleted. This is especially true during the last trimester, when your baby is rapidly growing. As you prepare your body for a healthy birth, seek out farmer's markets, small fruit and vegetable markets, and local farmers for delicious and healthy foods. By the time your baby is ready to eat solid foods, you will know where to find all the best ingredients.

A Whole-Foods Diet

What exactly are "whole foods"? Whole foods are those as close as possible to the form in which they were harvested from the earth. Nurturing yourself and your baby with these foods ensures that everything you eat is as full of nutrition as nature intended. There is a world of whole-food choices awaiting you and your baby, including a rainbow of fruits and vegetables, whole-grain pastas, breads and cereals, legumes, tofu, nuts and seeds, and organic chicken, eggs, fish, and lean meats. Whole foods can also be found in the form of high-quality oils such as organic, cold-pressed safflower, olive or sesame oils, and exotic sea vegetables such as hiziki and arame, which contain calcium that is more readily absorbed than that found in dairy products.

For vegetarians, eating a wide variety of whole foods will provide all the essential nutrients to nourish you and your developing baby. Choose nutrient-rich foods, and skip the empty calories. Include high-protein foods, healthy fats, and an abundance of fresh fruits and vegetables.

Whole grains

Brown rice and other whole grains (millet, oats, barley, and quinoa) are nutrient powerhouses full of vitamins, minerals, fiber, and protein. Because they are rich in complex carbohydrates, whole grains provide balanced energy and are calming. If you are not eating whole grains already, starting now will benefit both you and your child.

Healthy fats: omega-3 and omega-6 fatty acids

Omega-3 fatty acids are essential oils to nourish both you and your baby. You may have heard of docosahexaenoic acid (DHA), one of the essential oils found in fish; this oil is important for Baby's prenatal and postnatal neurodevelopment. Good fish choices that are lower in contaminants include herring, wild salmon, sardines, and Pacific halibut. Try to eat at least 1 tablespoon of herring oil or other high-quality fish oil daily. For those who want a plant-based source of these fatty acids (alpha-linoleic acid [ALA]), consume freshly ground organic flaxseed or flaxseed oil, pumpkin seeds, or walnuts daily.

Many moms-to-be tend to consume too much polyunsaturated, hydrogenated, refined, and low-quality oils. Instead, choose high-quality *unrefined* sources, such as organic **cold-pressed** safflower, olive or sesame oils that contain high-quality omega-6 fatty acids. These oils will help to keep your nervous system calm, your insides lubricated, and your skin glowing.

Evening primrose oil and borage oil (omega-6 oils) contain gamma-linoleic acid (GLA), an essential fatty acid, and they are excellent essential oils; include these in your diet to help balance hormones and reduce inflammation.

Organic fresh nuts and seeds

Organic fresh nuts and seeds are bursting with healthy protein, fats, vitamins, and minerals. Enjoy them as quick nutritious snacks, and use them as a tasty boost for rice and stews. The best seeds are sesame, sunflower, and pumpkin; the best nuts are almonds, walnuts, and pecans. Munch on them fresh, or roast them yourself without salt or with a touch of good-quality sea or **Celtic** salt. Be careful of preroasted nuts because they may contain mold. Nuts and seeds can also be eaten as spreads or milks; tahini (a sesame seed spread) is an excellent source of calcium, as is fresh almond milk.

Dark-green leafy vegetables

Kale and broccoli are excellent natural sources of calcium and some essential fatty acids (ALA). Eat them often.

Dairy products

During pregnancy and while nursing, choose organic dairy products. Conventional dairy products can contain traces of antibiotics, hormones, and pesticides. If you do not care for dairy products, calcium can be obtained from other sources, such as dark-green leafy vegetables, nuts and seeds, and sea vegetables.

Milk is more digestible warm, and some moms discover the added benefit of a more restful sleep when they drink it at bedtime with a pinch of nutmeg or turmeric. Goat's milk is more digestible than cow's milk, and it can also be brought to a light boil and drunk warm.

Meat

Poultry and red meat (in moderation) are good sources of the proteins that are essential during pregnancy. As with dairy, organic meat is best, and it is becoming increasingly available. Organic meat comes from animals that are not given antibiotics or growth hormones. Free-range organic, a method of farming in which animals are allowed to roam freely and are not kept in tight quarters, is the best choice.

Fish

We have all learned that fish is a nutritious food, high in healthy omega-3 fatty acid and protein. Lately, however, there have been many reports that some fish are not the best food choice because of mercury and PCB contamination. Pregnant women should avoid any fish that could contain these contaminants.

The safest fish to eat today are deepwater ocean fish such as Pacific halibut, tilapia, sole, wild salmon (Alaskan), black cod, sardines, herring, and canned pink sockeye. These recommended choices could change as the ocean's ecosystem changes, so it is important to stay informed on this issue. Some pregnant women choose to forgo fish altogether, whereas others eat only moderate servings of "clean" fish varieties.

Water

Now that you are pregnant, you may find that you are always thirsty. Water, nature's most vital nutrient, will keep you hydrated. Try to drink at least 2 liters of water daily. A tall glass of warm water every morning is the best-known remedy for constipation common during pregnancy.

LISTEN TO YOUR BODY

Now that you are pregnant, advice is plentiful. You may hear "Give in to your cravings," "Don't eat too much salt," "It's a boy if you crave," "Try not to gain too much weight," and "Go ahead and gain all the weight you want." Of all the advice pregnant moms receive, there is probably only one certainty—pregnancy is *not* a time to diet. Rather, it's a time to boost your intake of essential nutrients. Let food become a delight. Create a plan that includes some treats like cookies, but build it on a solid eating schedule.

Moms-to-be should always carry snacks so there is no need to resort to easily obtainable junk food when away from home. Good snacks to carry are raisins, dried fruit, nuts and seeds (almonds, sunflower, pumpkin), vegetable sticks, juices, crackers, fruits, and water. Eat often and never allow yourself to get too hungry. Small meals are better tolerated by the digestive system at this time.

Your body is going through many changes as a new life grows inside you. Mother's intuition starts right here. Listen to your body, and it will instinctively tell you what it needs. Your cravings may be a sign that your body needs a specific nutrient. For example, craving lots of ice cream or other dairy products may indicate your body's need for protein and calcium. If you crave ice cream, that is fine, but choose organic low-fat varieties and eat in moderation. Every mom-to-be will have her own personal cravings: some will be soothing, some physical, and others for pure enjoyment.

During pregnancy women can become sensitive to strong colors, sights, smells, and sounds, and they often experience morning sickness.

Many women ask: "How can I eat well when I am always nauseous?" The solution is to eat small, high-protein meals throughout the day, keeping something in your stomach at all times. Dry crackers, grapes, watermelon, and ginger work wonders for nausea, and grapefruit can help increase a diminished appetite.

Don't worry if you can't always eat properly; look forward to feasting in the second trimester. As the nausea of the first trimester typically eases, you will make up for lost calories. You'll need about 300 more calories a day to support your baby's growth. Nurture yourself by relaxing to enjoy the life blossoming inside of you. Get enough light exercise (not a time for hard core aerobics): yoga, meditation, nature walks, dance, tai chi, or swimming (in nonchlorinated, saltwater pools) are best.

VEGETARIAN CRAVINGS

As your baby draws from your nutrient stores, food cravings arise. Vegetarian moms might crave red meat, fish, or poultry when pregnant, if they ate these foods in the past. Many people's bodies take years to adjust to a vegetarian diet, so cravings for meat can still occur. You may be craving the concentrated protein in meat, and this may be a signal to increase your protein intake with whole grains such as quinoa and amaranth, or to eat more nuts and seeds.

In addition, nursing babies require significant amounts of vitamin B_{12}, which could lead to cravings for animal-based foods. Small amounts of organic animal products may do the trick if you desire; or consult with a nutritionist who can help you balance your vegetarian diet.

> ## We all need a treat
> High-quality dark chocolate containing at least 70 percent cocoa has recently been praised for its magnesium and

antioxidants. Small amounts of good organic dark chocolate can satisfy your chocolate craving in a healthy way.

Vitamins and Minerals

As your baby continues to grow, she needs a constant supply of vitamins and minerals. Most are available in supplement form, but they are also abundant in natural foods.

Folic acid

Folic acid, a B vitamin that aids B_{12} in developing a healthy spinal cord, is recommended before conception and should be taken throughout pregnancy (400 mcg daily).

Foods rich in folic acid

squash	romaine lettuce
lentils	orange juice
legumes	spinach
dark-green vegetables	wheat germ
egg yolks	tofu
apricots	liver

Iron

Iron is also important for keeping both mother and baby healthy. Enjoy foods high in iron, whether plant based or animal based (better absorbed), and have your blood checked for iron throughout your pregnancy. Pregnancy is the time to transfer optimum iron stores to your baby; she'll rely on these for at least six months after birth. Another goal of proper iron intake is to prevent anemia in the mother, which is common during pregnancy and after birth. You should also consider increasing your intake of iron because some blood will be lost during labor.

Foods rich in iron

beef	blackstrap molasses
liver	seaweed
lamb	dried fruit (especially apricots)
poultry	legumes
egg yolks	lentils
vegetables	seeds
whole grains	green leafy vegetables
iron-fortified grains	

Calcium

Calcium and magnesium are special minerals necessary to develop Baby's bones and nervous system. Babies will take what they need while in the womb, and they often draw these minerals from the mother's bones if her supplies are inadequate. Be sure to include foods high in calcium in your diet, or take a good-quality calcium, magnesium, and vitamin D supplement. Protecting your bones will also help prevent osteoporosis, which is so prevalent today. Some moms find that when taken at bedtime, calcium and magnesium supplements help with sleep and muscle cramps.

Foods rich in calcium

salmon with bones	almonds
dark-green leafy vegetables	beans

Many moms-to-be become deficient in chromium, causing sugar lows and intense sugar cravings. Balance your sugar levels by making sure that adequate amounts of chromium are contained in your daily supplement.

SUPPLEMENTS

Now that you are feeding two (or more), and your diet may not always be complete, a high-quality maternal vitamin supplement can help provide all your essential nutrients. It should contain adequate amounts of folic acid, iron, and chromium.

Other supplements you may want to consider include
- Calcium
- Magnesium
- Vitamin D
- B_{12} (recommended for vegetarian moms to prevent anemia)
- Probiotics (acidophilus and bifidus). Probiotics are beneficial intestinal flora that replenish healthy bacteria in the abdomen, especially if you experienced a lot of morning sickness in the first trimester.

Algae is a hot supplement today, in forms such as blue-green and spirulina. Many people consider these superfoods, but, as with any supplement, they should be treated as medicine and not be self-prescribed. Many sources of algae are polluted and could be toxic for you and your baby. Also, some algae have cleansing effects on your body, which is not good because pregnancy is a time to build and nourish. Pregnancy and lactation are not times to introduce new programs because not all their effects may be known. However, if you have been using a supplement such as pure spirulina for over a year, your doctor may give the okay.

Raspberry leaf tea is good in the last three to four weeks of pregnancy because it strengthens the uterus and reproductive system preparing for delivery. However, herbal remedies are medicines that can easily travel to the fetus. Always check with your doctor before taking them.

FOODS TO SKIP

Foods high in nitrates, sodium, and other additives should be avoided during your pregnancy. This includes deli meats, processed and deep-fried foods, refined sugar products, hydrogenated fats (trans fats), alcohol, and tobacco. Take a moment to read the ingredients to get into the habit of doing this for your baby. A good rule of thumb is that if you cannot pronounce the ingredient, it is probably not good for you. Refined sugar or grains can deplete your body of vital B vitamins. Healthier sweeteners include brown rice syrup, barley malt, pure maple syrup, pure stevia (green), and molasses (rich in iron). Artificial sweeteners found in soda pop and gum are not healthy.

Part II: Nutrition during Lactation

You and your baby will thrive if you continue eating a whole-foods diet while nursing. As during pregnancy, nursing is not a time for crash dieting. It takes a lot of energy to produce milk, and new mothers need to consume an extra 500 calories per day. Nursing will cause you to lose some of those extra maternal fat stores and may tire you out.

Moms producing good-quality milk should be hungry. If Mom is not producing sufficient milk, this may be an indicator that her body has not recuperated from childbirth, that she needs rest, or that she is not eating enough.

This nutrition plan for nursing moms is low in saturated fats and includes whole grains, fruits and vegetables, legumes, nuts and seeds, and moderate amounts of good fats. A poor diet when producing milk can deplete you of your mineral stores and rob your bones of calcium. As nursing babies take what they need from you, you should continue taking your prenatal vitamins. In particular, vegan moms will almost certainly require a vitamin B_{12} supplement to prevent their babies from becoming deficient.

A good breakfast is the best way to fuel you up for the day. Scrumptious smoothies, fruit blenders, and power breakfasts (muesli, oatmeal, and flax porridge) can all be found in the recipe section of this book. Continue energizing yourself throughout the day with high-protein grains such as quinoa and legumes.

NUTRITION TIPS FOR NURSING MOMS

- Do not eat on the run.
- Chew your food well to improve your digestion.
- For dairy products, remember that goat's milk is easier to digest than cow's milk.
- Include essential fatty acids daily (see pages 27–28).
- Keep healthy snacks close by and in your purse ready to go.
- Lactation consultants can be a great help if you are having trouble nursing. They can be found through your doctor, through breast-feeding clinics in your local hospital, or through La Leche League.

TIPS FOR INCREASING BREAST MILK

- Make sure that you rest when the baby does because tired and stressed moms produce lower-quality milk.
- Drink lots of fluids and have water close by each time you nurse.
- Eat a nutritionally balanced diet to keep up the quality of your milk.
- Some herbal supplements may increase milk supply, but because herbal remedies are not standardized and affect each person differently, you must consult with your physician before self-prescribing any of these.
- Nursing on demand when baby is hungry makes more milk, so the more you nurse, the more milk you produce.

- Eating the gruel on top of oatmeal and brown rice has also been shown to help.

Questions and Answers for Nursing Moms

What should I drink when nursing?

Water, the elixir of life, is the healthiest fluid choice (you should drink at least 2 liters of water per day). Fruit juices that have been diluted, fresh vegetable juices, and herbal teas also make good choices. Have a drink beside you every time you sit down to nurse. Avoid dehydrating beverages such as coffee, alcohol, and black teas.

Will the caffeine in my morning coffee pass through to my milk?

Yes, in approximately half an hour. Decaffeinated coffees still contain some caffeine, as do black teas. If you must have the odd coffee, make sure that it is not before the important morning feeding when your milk is plentiful and nutritious after your night's rest. If you must drink coffee, wait until after the first feeding and long before the next to reduce the caffeine in your milk.

We had a party last night and I'm afraid that I drank too much wine.

The younger your infant is, the more sensitive he or she will be to substances such as caffeine and alcohol. Take this into consideration, and limit your consumption to zero or to minimal amounts. Babies' sensitive organs, particularly the liver, will have the added burden of detoxifying any consumption of alcohol or recreational drugs. A little *nonalcoholic* beer on occasion has been shown to increase the quantity of breast milk in some women.

Can your diet affect your breast milk?

Of course! While you were pregnant, it may have been difficult to see how the foods you ate directly affected your baby, but now that you are nursing you will certainly be aware. Babies have immature digestive systems and can be sensitive to certain tastes. Each baby is unique; some infants are not supersensitive to what the mother eats, whereas others will not feed after the mother has eaten certain foods.

Culprit foods include onion, garlic, extremely spicy foods, and gassy foods such as cauliflower, cabbage, or broccoli. Nursing mothers who eat these foods may produce milk that will not be tolerated by the baby and that will give Baby stomach cramps. A diet including heavily fried foods and other unhealthy fats may cause your baby to have diarrhea or green stools.

For sensitive babies, keeping a diary of what you eat before a feeding can help you track down possible causes. If you suspect a food of being intolerable to your baby, try it again and monitor your baby's reaction, unless the first reaction was severe. Extreme reactions could be allergenic in nature, with symptoms such as hives or rashes, eczema, constipation or diarrhea, mucous, or congestion.

What type of fats should I be eating when nursing?

Omega-3 fats should be consumed every day so both you and your baby can receive their benefits. These fats are present in flax oil, freshly ground flaxseeds, and high-quality fish such as herring. The most important omega-3 fatty acid for brain development is docosahexaenoic acid (DHA), which is also found in fatty fish such as salmon, tuna, halibut, sardines, and trout. Some studies have shown that omega-3 fats help remedy postpartum depression as the new mother's brain is supplied with these essential fats.

> ## Interesting note
> Some researchers have established that a baby's future taste preferences may be determined by what the mother eats while nursing and possibly by what she eats even earlier, during pregnancy. Many moms can recall certain foods that they craved and ate frequently during pregnancy that now have become their child's favorites. That could be pickles or salty foods for one baby and sweet foods for another.

MEDICATIONS

Mothers who are taking any medications should consult with their pediatrician before beginning to nurse, because medications can pass through breast milk. Never take over-the-counter remedies, including herbal formulas, without consulting your pediatrician first. If you are having a problem, seek the help of a reliable health professional because this is not a time to self-diagnose. The answer could be as simple as extra bed rest. Remember that your breast milk changes throughout the day and is affected by your energy levels, diet, and eating schedule.

AROMATHERAPY FOR MOM

Aromatherapy is an effective, natural way to soothe the body and mind. If you have a cold you may find relief by steaming yourself with essential oils such as eucalyptus or lavender. Simply fill a bowl with boiling water, add the oils, place a towel around you and the bowl, and breathe the healing vapors in. You can energize yourself with a few drops of essential oil in the shower (but never put essential oils on your breasts because Baby will ingest them). Relax with lavender or sweet orange in a diffuser or with a few drops on your pillow or mixed with oil in your bath. These scents are great for Baby too.

chapter 2

A Journey to the Milky Way
Baby's First Six Months

"There is no finer investment for any community than putting milk into babies."

—Winston Churchill

NURSING

If you are able, nursing is the most natural and time-proven method for feeding babies. Breast milk is often imitated; it has never been duplicated. None of today's trendy and expensive baby formulas meet its superior nutritional qualities.

Many factors might influence your feelings about nursing, such as advertising, family, and cultural pressures. Perhaps looking to nature can offer some guidance. Newborn animals have different biological characteristics than newborn humans. Fish swim right after they are born, horses stand immediately after birth, and calves grow quickly. Our babies, on the other hand, are completely helpless and dependent upon us for many months after birth. It is as if nature intended mothers and babies to continue to share an emotional and nurturing connection outside the womb through nursing.

Nutritionally, breast milk is best for babies because

- It contains two amazing essential fatty acids, docosahexaenoic acid (DHA) and arachidonic acid (AA) that are essential for babies' brain and eye development
- Colostrum, the first milk after birth, is rich in antibodies, protein, minerals, and vitamins A, E, and B_{12}
- Mother's natural antibodies are transferred to the baby, which provides additional immunity and protection against infection
- Babies are rarely allergic to it and the likelihood of future food allergies may be reduced
- Babies are less likely to develop colic or gas because breast milk is easily digested
- Nursed babies experience little constipation, diarrhea, or spitting up
- Nursing reinforces bonds between mother and baby
- Nursing promotes natural development of the mouth, leading to stronger jaw and teeth formation
- Nursed babies get fewer ear infections
- Iron in breast milk is easily absorbed (bioavailable)
- Nursing allows for superb mineral absorption
- The taste and nutritional content of mother's milk cannot be duplicated in the lab
- Breast milk is convenient, allowing babies to feed anytime, always at the right temperature
- Dirty diapers smell sweet

Risk factors a nursing mother should consider

There are some risk factors that could complicate breastfeeding or should preclude a mother from breastfeeding altogether, including HIV infection, drug addiction, breast implants, or general illness. Consult your pediatrician before breastfeeding if you think you may fall into any of these categories.

Historically, the people of many different cultures have felt that breastfeeding was so important that they had wet nurses in their villages. These women were carefully selected and may have nursed several babies at a time.

Signs of a thriving breastfed baby

With bottle-fed babies, you can easily see how many ounces of milk have been consumed. Some signs that a nursed baby has eaten enough include

- Baby is satisfied after feeding and may drift off to sleep
- Baby regains birth weight within a couple of weeks
- Baby (on an average) wets six diapers and has three bowel movements per day
- Baby continues to gain weight and grow
- You are able to stretch out the time between feedings

BABY'S DIGESTIVE SYSTEM

A baby's digestive system is not fully developed until about two years of age. The lining of a baby's small intestine is very permeable to large proteins during the first six months of life. This allows protective antibodies found in breast milk to be readily absorbed into the baby's bloodstream. After six months of age, babies begin to produce their own antibodies, and their small intestine becomes much less permeable to proteins. Therefore, proteins (other than those found in breast milk), if given too early in too large a quantity, can cause changes in the gut lining, leading to vital nutrients such as calcium leaching out.

Although this permeability during the first six months is great for boosting immunity to disease, a downside is that it allows proteins from potentially allergenic foods to pass directly into Baby's blood. This can, in some cases, lead to the early development of food allergies, or even to cell damage in the digestive tract.

Babies younger than six months do not produce all of the necessary enzymes to properly digest complex foods, such as fats, starches, and certain proteins. Levels of some digestive enzymes do not reach "adult" levels until a child reaches two years of age. Feeding babies certain foods too early can lead to digestive problems such as bloating, gas, cramps, and diarrhea.

It is recommended that only breast milk (or approved infant formula) be fed for the first six months. Foods containing complex animal proteins (meat and dairy products) should be delayed until around ten months and some vegetable proteins, such as nuts, until even later. Some physicians have recently suggested introducing meats to babies as young as six months, to prevent iron deficiency. However, the whole-foods diet presented here provides plenty of easily absorbed iron for your baby and is easy on digestion.

Solid foods before six months?

Consult your pediatrician first if you want to start your baby on solid foods at four to six months. If your child is ready for solids at this age, green and orange vegetable purees can be introduced at four to six months, along with brown rice grain milk and mashed banana. Ideally, cereals should not be introduced until around six months, when Baby's digestive system is stronger. Waiting until six months to introduce cereals can help prevent the development of food allergies.

Healthy Foods for Four to Six Months ✿

- Breast milk
- Brown rice grain milk
- Mashed banana

First green vegetable purees

- Peas
- Green beans

Sweet orange vegetable purees

- Butternut squash puree
- Sweet potato puree

Dental Care

Caring for your baby's teeth begins soon after birth, even though those pearly whites are still hiding under the gums. Primary teeth can erupt starting around six months of age (sometimes earlier), are kept until about six years of age, and are essential for chewing food and as placeholders for adult teeth. Healthy gums and primary teeth are a good foundation for the permanent teeth that will follow.

By following a simple cleaning procedure starting a few days after birth, you can establish a routine for caring for your baby's teeth and his beautiful smile. After each feeding, wet a clean, soft washcloth or gauze pad and gently wipe your baby's gums, inside the cheeks, roof of the mouth, and tongue. Also, make sure to clean Baby's gums before bedtime, because bacteria can cause damage during sleep.

How's Baby Growing?

Your pediatrician will regularly monitor your baby's general health and behavior throughout the first six months. Key points that pediatricians pay attention to at this time include

- **Appetite:** Is Baby's appetite strong or poor? Is there excessive hunger or thirst?
- **Skin:** Are Baby's cheeks bright and is his overall color good? Also checks for rashes, bumps, hives, eczema, and dry skin.
- **Eyes:** Are Baby's eyes bright and clear, not dull?
- **Bowel movements:** Checks for color, consistency, and frequency.
- **Digestive system:** Is Baby colicky or gassy?
- **Sleeping patterns:** Does Baby sleep a lot, on a regular cycle? Or does he wake frequently?
- **Baby's disposition:** Is Baby calm and happy? Or is he hyper or colicky?
- **Alertness:** Is Baby attentive, with good focus? Is baby listless?
- **Weight:** Is Baby gaining weight and height steadily? Monitor if Baby is underweight or overweight.
- **Breathing:** Should be gentle and even, not mucus-sounding, heavy, or gasping.
- **Immune system:** Have there been many infections and fever, or earache? Is there a family history of allergies?

Although these points can help determine if your baby is healthy and well nourished, parents' common sense is also important. Every baby develops differently; for example, some are simply genetically smaller than others. Appreciate your baby's unique nature and do not attempt to rush milestones, as they will all be reached in due course.

I WANT TO KNOW! SEVEN COMMONLY ASKED QUESTIONS.

How much breast milk does my baby need?

All babies' needs are different; some have a higher activity level, some may be going through a growth spurt or were born premature. Babies know intuitively when they are full or when they need more food and tend to drink more than enough milk to support their growth.

Do I have to nurse for one year?

No, but the longer you nurse, the more benefits your baby will receive. Many doctors now advocate nursing up until one year if possible, but for a minimum of six months.

I'm going back to work after four weeks of breast-feeding. What do I do?

Today's reality is that many moms work, and maternity leave is limited. For those who do not want to pump, any period of breastfeeding is more beneficial than none. Many work places now accommodate new mothers with day care and flexible hours. Pumping and storing milk is also an alternative so that a caregiver can feed your baby.

Can your diet affect your breast milk?

Yes. Just as antibodies were transferred through your milk to your baby in the first few days, your baby will also receive the things you eat through your milk. Some babies are hypersensitive and may fuss about overly spicy, sour, or bitter-tasting milk and prefer their moms to have a blander diet; others are quite hardy, bothered by nothing mom eats. Choose foods wisely because everything you eat, including caffeine, herbs, and medicines, goes through breast milk. A journal can be used to record what you eat and how your baby reacts. (See Chapter 1 for more information on lactation.)

Do babies need extra water?

Because both breast milk and formula are about 90 percent water, usually no additional water is necessary if Baby is nursing enough, at least until solids are introduced and milk is reduced. In hot climates, such as Texas in the summer, babies can occasionally become dehydrated and may need extra water. Pediatricians will tell you to be concerned about dehydration when your baby has not had a wet diaper in about eight hours and seems irritable.

Does my baby need a vitamin D supplement?

Babies need appropriate amounts of vitamin D, a nutrient essential for calcium absorption. It helps prevent a rare condition called rickets, in which the body takes calcium out of the bones to perform its important functions.

Breast milk contains minute amounts of vitamin D, and babies are born with some stores (unless the mother was deficient in this vitamin during pregnancy). Infant formulas are supplemented with enough vitamin D to meet a baby's needs. Mothers feeding their babies a fifty-fifty combination of breast milk and formula will probably be advised that their baby is receiving enough vitamin D.

Though a vitamin D supplement is recommended by the American Academy of Pediatrics for breastfed infants, pediatricians are divided on this issue. One opinion is that a supplement is necessary and another opinion is that babies get enough vitamin D from regular exposure to the sun. In extreme northern climates such as Alaska or northern Canada, a supplement may be necessary. Your doctor will determine what is necessary for your baby.

Does breast milk contain enough iron?

Most babies are born with iron stores that last from four to six months. For babies who are exclusively nursed, their iron stores are supplemented by breast milk, which although low in iron, is easily absorbed. The introduction of solid foods will bring new sources of iron. Premature babies' iron stores may deplete before solids are introduced. In all cases, you should consult your physician on the need for a supplement.

Choosing an infant formula

The most common infant formulas are cow's milk based or soy based. To date, none of these have matched breast milk. If you are using formula, your pediatrician will determine which formula is best for your baby.

Unacceptable formulas include regular store-bought cow's milk, evaporated (canned) milk, goat, soy, rice, or almond milks. Cow's milk in particular is an unsuitable substitute for breast milk because of its very different composition and allergenic nature. Store-bought milks, especially soy and almond, can be highly allergenic and do not contain enough protein or fat to allow the baby to thrive. Goat's milk is more easily digested than cow's milk, but does not make a suitable infant formula as it is deficient in folic acid and iron.

"We can do no great things; only small things with great love."

—Mother Theresa

chapter 3

Building Blocks for Baby Nutrition

"Vitamin trouble," Stuart replied. *"She took vitamin D when she needed A. She took vitamin B when she was short of C, and her system became overloaded with riboflavin, thiamine hydrochloride, and pyridoxine, the need for which in human nutrition has not yet been established."*

—From *Stuart Little,* by E. B. White (1945)

Mother's milk contains the perfect proportion of carbohydrates, proteins, fats, vitamins, and minerals to fuel your growing child, and formula mirrors this as closely as humanly possible. Before long, your baby will be getting many of her essential nutrients from solid food. This chapter will tell you all you need to know about the building blocks necessary to make your child strong and healthy.

CARBOHYDRATES: FUEL ME UP!

Carbohydrates (good versus bad) are always in the news—what's so special about them? They are the preferred source of energy for the whole body including the brain and central nervous system. They are of two types, simple and complex, though both eventually become glucose in the bloodstream.

Complex carbohydrates, the "good" carbohydrates, are found in whole foods such as whole-grain cereals, breads and pastas, legumes, fruits, and vegetables. As they take longer to digest than their simple friends, they provide babies with a constant source of energy to fuel their growth, particularly when they begin to crawl and walk.

Simple carbohydrates are digested quickly and contribute to sugar highs and lows (a seesaw of energy) that can leave your child irritable and without energy. Some simple carbohydrates, such as those found in brown rice syrup, rice and barley malt, pure maple syrup, molasses, and honey, are okay (after the first year) in small amounts. Highly refined carbohydrates such as white table sugar, corn syrup, refined grain products, and refined sweets have been stripped of their natural nutrients and are not recommended. Complex carbohydrates are best because simple ones fill your child with empty calories, and in excess they can deplete the body's source of B vitamins.

Never use artificial sweeteners in place of sugar, because babies have a hard time digesting these chemical substances.

PROTEINS: BUILDING YOUR BABY

Protein is vital for babies' growth and repair. Babies need protein for every process in the body, including hair, muscles, and enzymes for digestion. Proteins also help babies resist infection and build strong immune systems. Breast milk is the best source of protein to fuel your baby's rapid growth during the first year.

Protein is composed of twenty-two amino acids that either come from food or are produced in our body. Complete proteins contain all the amino acids needed for growth. Animal sources such as eggs, poultry, and meat are complete proteins. Soy is also a complete protein.

Baby's digestive system easily absorbs plant-based protein. Proteins from plant sources such as quinoa are easily digestible for babies and highly absorbable. Superb plant-based proteins include legumes, grains (millet, amaranth), seeds and nuts, green leafy vegetables, and sprouted seeds. When eaten in combination these foods provide complete proteins.

Animal sources of protein are harder for Baby to digest, so use these foods in small quantities only.

FATS: THEY'RE NOT ALL BAD

All of the conflicting information surrounding fats has led us to confusion. The truth about fats is that babies need them for growth and brain development. The confusion is between good fats and bad fats.

Good fats include the monounsaturated fats prevalent in olive, peanut, canola, or rapeseed oils, avocado, and polyunsaturated fats such as omega-3 and omega-6. Omega-3 fatty acids are highly concentrated in fatty fish such as salmon, sardines, mackerel, and anchovies, and other fish such as tuna. Plant-based omega-3 sources are green leafy vegetables, flaxseed (the absolute best), soybeans, and walnuts. Omega-6 oils are primarily found in sunflower, safflower, corn, and soybean oils.

Bad fats are saturated and trans fats. Too many saturated fats in childhood have been implicated as a cause of eczema, asthma, and other inflammatory diseases such as arthritis and heart disease, which cause elevated blood cholesterol. Saturated fats are mostly found in animal products such as meat, poultry, seafood, whole milk, butter, cheese, and eggs. Plant-based foods that contain large amounts of saturated fats are coconut and palm oils.

Trans fats are man-made, produced by a process called hydrogenation. Snack and convenience foods containing trans fats include margarines, potato chips, manufactured cookies, cakes, microwave popcorn, granola bars, and processed food such as frozen pizzas and fish sticks.

Healthy fats

- provide a concentrated energy source with twice the calories of an equal amount of carbohydrate or protein.
- are necessary for the absorption, transportation, and digestion of the fat-soluble vitamins (A, D, E, and K).
- play a crucial role in the development of the brain and eyes. In the brain, they help to encase the myelin sheath (the nerves' protective coating), and in the eye, they help develop the light-sensitive cells of the retina.
- are essential for maintaining a normal balance of sugar in the bloodstream.
- contain essential fatty acids, such as omega-3 and omega-6, that cannot be made in the body.
- protect and cushion babies' developing bodies and their internal organs.

Babies thrive on the full healthy fats found in breast milk, which comprise over 50 percent of breast milk's calories. Beyond breast milk, feed your baby good fats that are monounsaturated and polyunsaturated, and only the smallest amounts of saturated fat. Avoid feeding your baby any trans fats.

> Babies' and toddlers' diets should not restrict the intake of healthy fats before the age of two. Whole fats should provide roughly half of their calories.

CHOLESTEROL

Cholesterol is a lipid, not a fat, and is not an energy source for the body. However, it is vital for our bodily processes and, like fats, has both good and bad forms. For babies it aids in the production of vitamin D, assists in the absorption of calcium for strong bones, is a part of the myelin sheath that encases nerve cells, and is involved in digestion.

Dietary cholesterol is found in animal products, but as the liver produces all the cholesterol we need, our intake of animal foods must be moderate. Studies have shown that some children as early as four years old have high cholesterol levels, primarily a result of diets too high in saturated fats.

WATER

Breastfed babies generally get enough water from their mother's milk. Bottle-fed babies may need to be given tiny amounts of water because formula may cause them to become thirsty. A baby's body is about 75 percent water and proper hydration is vital to all bodily functions.

All babies need water after solid foods are introduced to aid in digestion and elimination. In very hot weather some breastfed babies may require additional water. Carbonated mineral water is not suitable for babies because it can cause gas and cramping.

FIBER

Fiber is essentially a complex carbohydrate that is indigestible. It helps prevent constipation, a common problem in children, and can also lower the risk of heart disease, diabetes, and irritable bowel. Plant-based foods such as whole grains, fruits, vegetables, dried fruits, and legumes are fiber-rich foods for your toddler.

Given the small size of babies' and toddlers' tummies, too much fibrous, bulky food can fill them up before they have consumed enough calories or other nutrients. This may be of concern in some vegetarian babies. Too much fiber can also cause diarrhea, gas, and stomachaches.

SALT

Salt helps babies maintain fluid balance and is needed for nerve formation. Babies' whose nutrition comes primarily from breast milk and/or formula will receive an adequate supply of salt. Older babies will obtain natural salts from fruits, vegetables, whole grains, and sea vegetables.

Babies' diets are naturally bland and do not need extra salt during the first year. Because adults have a seasoned palate, they may want to add salt to Baby's food after tasting it. This is a mistake. What is bland for an adult is perfect for a baby. Too much salt can stress a baby's kidneys and cause the development of a salty palate at an early age. Also, the addition of extra salt to their diets may slow a baby's growth.

After one year, tiny amounts of high-quality sea salt may be used in cooking. Avoid refined table salt, which is devoid of all the necessary minerals.

SUGAR

Breast milk is naturally sweet and provides the best sugar for babies. Babies also thrive on the naturally occurring sugars found in vegetables, fruits, and whole grains. After beginning solids, whole-grain cereals can be sweetened with breast milk or tiny amounts of organic rice syrup, rice malt, or barley malt to continue the natural sweetness from breast milk that babies love. Honey, corn syrup, or maple syrup should not be given in the first year, as there is a risk of infant botulism (severe food poisoning).

Feeding your baby natural sugars like those in fruit emphasizes healthy habits. Stay away from highly refined sugars found in processed foods.

PHYTONUTRIENTS: GOODNESS FROM THE EARTH

As they are increasing in popularity, you may have heard about phytonutrients, the naturally occurring nutrients found in plants. Many of these substances, such as lycopene (from tomatoes) and beta-carotene (from carrots and sweet potatoes) have proven health benefits. Vegetables often contain thousands of phytonutrients. Grains are nutrient-dense foods that contain phytonutrients in their natural forms. Supplements cannot duplicate all of the phytonutrients found in a single tomato.

VITAMINS AND MINERALS

Whole, natural foods can provide your baby with all the essential vitamins and minerals necessary for growth. Breast milk or formula provides Baby with the first vitamins and minerals, and later a well-balanced diet will continue to nourish Baby. Processed foods are highly refined and often depleted of nutrients; some nutrients are added back when fortified— however, they never match nature's forms.

Vitamin A

Vitamin A promotes healthy eyesight, enhances immunity, and assists in forming strong bones, gums, and teeth. Good sources for babies include carrots, squash, cantaloupe, mango, dried apricots, sweet potato, and eggs.

B-complex vitamins

The B complex includes vitamins B_1 (thiamin), B_2 (riboflavin), B_3, B_5, B_6, B_{12}, and folic acid. These vitamins contribute to a wide variety of bodily functions, including nervous system development, digestion, immune system enhancement, and proper growth. Babies need appropriate amounts of each to thrive; a deficiency or excess of one B vitamin can disrupt the functioning of the whole group.

Good sources for ages six months to one year include whole-grain cereals and pastas, dark leafy greens, legumes, tofu, avocados, and bananas. Sources for ages one to two years include these and whole-grain breads, eggs, nuts, dairy products, meat, seeds, oily fish, and brewer's yeast.

A star performer in this group is vitamin B_{12}, which helps maintain a healthy nervous system and is needed in the formation of red blood cells and DNA. A serious vitamin B_{12} deficiency could cause pernicious anemia (decreased red blood cells in bone marrow) or even possible neurological damage. Strict vegetarians must supplement their diets with B_{12} because it is mainly found in animal products. A good source up to one year is yogurt. Up to age two years, other sources include eggs, meat, seafood, dairy products, and fortified breakfast cereals.

Folic acid

Folic acid (folacin) is essential in the manufacturing of red blood cells, DNA, and RNA. In the womb, growing babies use folic acid for proper brain and spinal cord development. A folic acid supplement should be taken by women before conception, during pregnancy, and after Baby's birth.

Good sources up to one year are dark-green leafy vegetables, dried fruit, apricots, legumes, and squash. For up to age two, egg yolks, romaine lettuce, nuts, whole wheat, avocado, and fortified cereals are good sources.

Vitamin C

Vitamin C is essential to promote the absorption of iron for the development of healthy immune systems, and as an antioxidant, for growth, tissue repair, and the formation of cartilage and muscles.

Good sources of vitamin C up to one year include fruit (in particular cantaloupe, kiwi, papaya, mangoes, and baby apple juice), sweet potato, bell peppers, squash, broccoli, and dark-green leafy vegetables. For ages one to two years, good sources include citrus fruits, strawberries, berries, tomatoes, and potatoes.

Vitamin D

Vitamin D is formed in the body when the skin is exposed to sunlight, and it assists in the absorption of calcium and phosphorous needed for strong bones and teeth. Babies and children who receive inadequate sunlight may need a vitamin D supplement, but pediatricians are divided as to whether breastfed infants need this supplement as well. Your pediatrician will be able to assess your baby's needs. Infant formulas contain sufficient amounts of vitamin D. Severe cases of vitamin D deficiency can result in rickets, which is characterized by soft and weak bones.

Good sources of vitamin D up to the age of one year include fish and fish oils, infant formulas, and sunlight. For ages one to two years, additional sources include fortified dairy products and cereals.

Vitamin E

Vitamin E helps protect cell membranes, is needed in red blood cells and fatty acids, and acts as an anticoagulant and antioxidant. Good sources up to one year include whole grains, dark-green leafy vegetables, and avocados. For babies between ages one and two, good sources include wheat germ, nuts and seeds, and healthy vegetable oils including cold-pressed olive, safflower, corn, and soybean.

Vitamin K

Newborns are usually given a vitamin K shot at birth to help prevent hemorrhage. It is important for blood clotting and for healthy bones. Good sources up to age one include dark-green leafy vegetables and yogurt. For ages one to two years, good sources include brussels sprouts, milk, egg yolks, and kelp.

Vitamin and mineral supplements for babies

Always check with your doctor before giving vitamin or mineral supplements to a baby or child and never give them adult formula supplements.

Iron

Babies have enough iron stores at birth to last for the first six months of life; after that they need to replenish them. (Babies' birth weight typically triples during their first year, as does their blood volume, hence their need for iron.) Generally, premature babies may deplete their iron stores a couple of months earlier because they do not have enough time to accumulate iron stores like their full-term cousins. Mom may have also been deficient in iron during her pregnancy.

After six months, breast milk and non-iron-fortified formula may not offer sufficient iron and zinc. Babies are more efficient at absorbing iron from breast milk than from cow's milk based infant formulas.

Iron is essential for the formation of red blood cells, which carry oxygen to all the cells in the body. Inadequate intake of iron could result in iron deficiency anemia, characterized by a child who lacks energy, gets frequent infections, has poor appetite, and is always cold. Vegetarian diets need to be closely monitored for iron, because plant-based sources are not as easily absorbable as animal sources. Pediatricians frequently check babies' iron levels at this time and may prescribe Baby iron supplements. Iron deficiency most commonly occurs between the first and second year.

Jessie loses her appetite

At around eight months, Jesse began to lose her appetite, nursing less and eating very little solid food. Jessie had been born one and a half months premature. Our pediatrician suggested a hemoglobin (protein in red blood cells) test to see if she was low in iron. Sure enough, she was low. An infant iron supplement restored her appetite in no time.

Good sources of iron for babies include whole-grain cereals, green leafy vegetables, seaweed, dried fruit (apricots), raisins, prunes, dates, lentils, legumes, seeds, iron-fortified infant cereals, and iron-fortified infant formula. For babies aged one to two years, all of the above foods plus meat, poultry, lamb, egg yolks, blackstrap molasses, beets, and nuts are good sources.

Calcium

Calcium is essential for the development of healthy bones, teeth, nerves, and muscles. Recent research suggests that calcium is so crucial during the first year of life that accumulating maximum calcium stores in bones during this time could help prevent osteoporosis later in life. Calcium in breast milk is readily absorbed, and helps to set a solid foundation for healthy bones. Accordingly, adequate calcium intake must be provided in the diet of children who do not consume dairy products.

Good sources of calcium for babies up to one year of age include breast milk, infant formula, green leafy vegetables, broccoli, sesame seeds, tofu, and yogurt. For babies aged one to two years, dairy products (milk and cheese), nuts (almonds), seeds (sunflower), salmon and sardines with bones, and soybeans are good sources.

Zinc

Zinc is a trace nutrient important for babies' growth and development, neurological functions, and to build strong immune systems. Breast milk is a good source of easily absorbed zinc, as are zinc-fortified formulas. Vegetarians need to make sure their babies get enough zinc because like iron, it is not as readily absorbed from plant sources. Children deficient in zinc may suffer from poor appetite, slower growth, and more frequent infections.

Good sources of zinc up to one year of age include breast milk, zinc-fortified formula, whole grains, zinc-enriched infant cereals, lentils, and legumes. For babies up to two years, good sources include whole grains, cheese and other dairy products, eggs, some nuts and seeds, red meat, tuna, and sardines.

Fluoride

Fluoride is a trace element typically added to municipal drinking water. It is important for the development of strong bones and, especially, teeth. You can find out the amount of fluoride in your local water supply by checking with your local water authority or public health department. Some well water and bottled water may not contain enough fluoride, and your pediatrician and dentist can advise you if your child needs a supplement. Note that too much fluoride is not good either, as it can cause discolored teeth or streaky white lines on teeth. A good source of fluoride is to cook with water that contains it.

> *"Let food be thy medicine, thy medicine shall be thy food."*
>
> —Hippocrates

chapter 4

A Journey to the Market

"Shipping is a terrible thing to do to vegetables.
They probably get jet-lagged, just like people."

—Elizabeth Berry

As a new parent, you may begin to look at things differently, thinking about future generations, perhaps your own grandchildren. What will the environment be like for them? What foods will they eat? As our oceans become more polluted, for example, the list of "safe to eat" fish grows shorter. These concerns usually begin in pregnancy when we notice neighbors spraying their lawn with pesticides, and wonder how it might affect our unborn child.

It is easy to be taken in by the vibrant colors and smells coming from supermarket produce. However, produce that has been shipped to your supermarket from far-off locales is sprayed with chemicals to preserve it for the journey. Oranges are picked green, sprayed, and left to ripen en route. Upon arrival, these oranges are a shocking orange color, at their peak of ripeness and irresistible. Left to ripen on the plants, these fruits would be loaded with nutrients, but would never make the journey. These chemicals are used to maximize crop yield, not nutrition. They often penetrate the porous skin of fruits and vegetables and reach the abundant nutrients that sit just below the skin.

Imagine a time in the past, when foods were organic, locally grown, and so fresh they were a treat for the senses; a time when people ate what they grew and shared food with their neighbors. Today, we eat food imported from all over the world, some of which is out of season for us. A trip to your local grocery store in search of healthy foods can send many people into a panic, as the selection can be overwhelming.

ORGANIC FOODS
Are organic foods nutritionally superior?

The debate as to whether organics foods are nutritionally superior is an important one. Some research says that organics are nutritionally superior to conventional products by two times and others say that although there is a difference, it is not significant. This aside, the fact remains that vitamins and minerals in organic produce are in their natural states, the food is grown in healthy soil, is not chemically altered or genetically modified, and is in a form easily absorbed by the body. And, clearly, organic produce does not carry with it the risk of pesticides and chemicals leaching into it and affecting nutrients just below the skin.

In North America, organic food is mostly grown according to regulated standards. In the case of farm produce, this means no artificial pesticides, chemical fertilizers, or food additives. In the case of animal products, it means the animal is raised in a humane environment without antibiotics and growth hormones.

Studies have shown that school-age children fed diets low in exposure to pesticides have much lower blood levels of pesticides such as organophosphates than those who ate nonorganically grown fruits, vegetables, and whole grains. It is believed that future research will confirm the significant nutritional benefits of organics.

Organics are chemical free

Wherever a baby goes, be it to the doctor's office or to see friends and relatives, germs and chemicals are everywhere. Babies' immature digestive systems cannot detoxify chemicals that are consumed, so it is particularly important to minimize these substances when it comes to Baby's first foods. Thankfully, the food we give our babies is the one area where we can control and minimize the pollutants and chemicals they encounter.

Organic foods, which are free of chemicals, are ideal at this time (at least for the first year though preferably beyond). Some foods such as root vegetables and banana are best eaten in their organic form at all times, as they easily absorb pesticides while growing.

If the widespread use of chemicals has not convinced you of the merits of organic foods, at least for your baby at this stage, the taste will. Organic produce may not always look as wonderful as nonorganic, particularly in colder climates during winter, but the taste is far better.

Choose wisely

Faced with two choices—an organic peach and a nonorganic, locally grown in-season peach—the organic peach may not always be the best choice. It is important to examine organic food carefully. Not all "organic" food is *truly* organic, as not every country has organic growing standards such as America. An "organic" peach brought in from far away may be no better than eating a local peach that is in season at home.

Organic produce in particular can have several shortcomings that are unrelated to nutrition but still important.

- Inconsistency: Some weeks the produce is wonderful and others it's not (unless you live in California where the growing season is year round).
- Scarcity in colder climates: Living in colder climates means less variety, especially when you are buying seasonally and locally.

- Bugs: Given the lack of pesticides, bugs are common in organic produce, which is why organic fruits and vegetables, particularly leafy greens, must be soaked and washed thoroughly before use.
- Shorter shelf life
- Slightly higher price

Yet in my opinion, none of these shortcomings offsets the nutritional and health benefits of organic foods for your baby. Organic foods are not only for the elite, although they do tend to be slightly more expensive than regular foods. Organics are far more affordable now than they ever were, and prices are still coming down as more producers switch to organic farming practices and more stores and markets stock organics to keep up with demand.

Prepared organic baby foods

Although homemade baby food is best, for those inevitable situations when you are in a jam and you need baby food quickly, there are prepared organic baby foods available. You can buy them in both jarred and frozen forms. In my opinion, the color, taste, and texture of the frozen versions are slightly better than jarred, although your baby might not like the taste or texture if he is used to homemade.

Even though the manufacturers of prepared organic baby foods may use organic ingredients, their processes are the same as any other manufacturer: high temperatures are used that impact the texture, color, and taste of the food. If you do not believe this, I suggest you try your own comparison test. Look at your own pureed green beans and compare them to the prepared brands. Yours will have a remarkable green color. Do a taste-test as well.

READING FOOD LABELS

Food in the United States is regulated by the Food and Drug Administration (FDA) and the United States Department of Agriculture Food

Safety and Inspection Services (USDA FDIS). These agencies are responsible for ensuring all food products are properly labeled with complete nutrition and ingredient information. Store-bought baby food is highly regulated and will not contain the additives found in foods for older children such as artificial sweeteners like aspartame that are frequently present in junk food (snacks such as cookies, chips, soda pop).

Food intended for children over three (which is when the FDA takes off its watch for babies) needs to be checked for "sugar" ingredients under many names such as glucose, fructose, lactose, sucrose, cane sugar, corn syrup, hydrolyzed starch, inverted sugar, dextrose, fruit juice concentrate, molasses, mannitol, maltose, honey, and high-fructose corn syrup. For further information visit the FDA website.

SKIP THE ADDITIVES

Get in the habit of reading food labels as early as during pregnancy. Be a detective, searching for the healthiest ingredients possible. Many long, almost unpronounceable, names on food labels often look like a different language. Additives may be used to preserve food, extend a product's shelf life, add tastes such as sweet or salty, or be "good for you" nutrients. Get to know which ingredients may be non-healthy chemical additives or nutritious ones such as the vitamin thiamin. Chances are that if you cannot pronounce it, it is not good for you.

The United States is the world's largest consumer of food additives, using somewhere around three thousand different additives. Recently, groundbreaking research has shown that food additives can cause adverse effects in children, such as hyperactivity. In addition, ingredients that add salt, such as monosodium glutamate (MSG) can put stress on a child's kidneys. With this in mind, the decision to serve your baby whole, natural, unprocessed foods free from preservatives is the right choice.

At the beginning of your baby's solid food journey, your choices are easy: organic whole grains, vegetables, and fruit. However, once Baby's diet becomes more varied, you may decide to buy some natural teething cookies or other whole-grain breads to make teething toast or other snack foods. That is where some grocery stores and natural food stores come into play, helping you to find the healthiest treats. Labels must be read carefully, as convenience foods can contain preservatives or additives that are unhealthy. This is another reason to stick with whole foods for your baby.

Prepared baby food packaging contains very simple labels that list carbohydrates, protein, fat, vitamin, mineral, sodium, and calorie content. They will also tell you the percentage of daily requirements of each nutrient in the jar. Never buy low-fat or nonfat products for babies because they need healthy whole fats for brain development.

FOOD SAFETY TIPS

1. When possible, buy seasonal local produce or grow your own.
2. Peeling will reduce the amount of pesticides in nonorganic fruits and vegetables, but it will not entirely eliminate them. In particular, pesticides are highly concentrated in apples, peaches, pears, grapes, oranges, green beans, green peas, carrots, and potatoes.
3. Use deepwater ocean white fish and avoid fish from lakes that could be polluted. Always check the local information for fish that are safest to eat.
4. Root vegetables such as carrots, beets, spinach, and turnip greens contain nitrates from the soil, so use organic varieties and in moderation for the first eight months. Baby food manufactures do not allow nitrates in prepared baby food.
5. "Irradiated" food is food that is radiated to kill bacteria and extend shelf life. The effects of this process are inconclusive, so these foods are not recommended for babies. Check your food for an irradiation label, as some packaging now contains one.
6. Avoid genetically modified foods (GMOs), as they are developed in laboratories to yield supercrops at less cost. It has not been

established that they are nutritionally superior. Given the controversy surrounding GMOs, most baby food manufacturers do not use them.

7. Choose organic beef that is free of Bovine Growth Hormone (BGH). BGH is injected into cows to make them produce more milk and is banned in Canada and Europe.

8. Never use dishes made from polyvinyl chloride (PVC) in the microwave. When heated, they can release harmful chemicals that may be absorbed into the food. Only use certified microwave-safe dishes, preferably glass or ceramic.

A COLORFUL MOSAIC OF FOODS

When you are at the market, choose from a wide variety of colorful fruits and vegetables. Include many different colors in this mosaic of foods and you will give your child a better selection of the nutrients he needs to grow.

Red

beets	strawberries
tomatoes	red cabbage
watermelon	red bell peppers
cherries	red apples
raspberries	

Orange

carrots	apricots
sweet potatoes	papaya
yams	mango
squash	orange bell peppers
oranges	melon
peaches	

Yellow

corn	bananas
yellow bell peppers	pineapple
yellow plums	

Green

broccoli	peas
green pepper	limes
asparagus	avocado
zucchini	granny smith apples
cucumber	dark leafy greens (kale, bok choy, spinach, collards)

Blue

blueberries	raisins
grapes	figs

Purple

plums	eggplant
blackberries	

White

onions	garlic
cauliflower	parsnips

FOOD AND THE SEASONS

Take some guidance from the ancient civilizations of Asia, and try to feed your baby in tune with the seasons (once he is eating solids). Each season, you should try to nourish and strengthen specific organs, but remember to only serve foods that are acceptable for your baby's age at a given time. Always serve fruit at room temperature, neither hot nor cold. Some examples:

Winter: Nourish the kidney and bladder; serve no cold drinks and more cooked food than raw. Great foods include root vegetable stew, squash, hearty grains (such as brown rice and buckwheat), legumes (such as kidney and adzuki beans), and very small amounts of seaweed (such as kombu). After age one, miso soup may be introduced.

Spring: Nourish the liver and gallbladder. Suggested foods include grains such as barley, spring greens, and lighter vegetables.

Summer: Nourish the heart and small intestines. Great foods include watermelon, locally grown fruits and vegetables, corn, and strawberries (both after one year).

Autumn: Nourish the lungs and large intestines. Great foods include fall vegetables (kale, broccoli, onion, and leeks) and local fruit (apples and pears).

> A diet that is high in whole grains, fruits and vegetables, and legumes and seeds, with small amounts of animal products, supports our environment and keeps us nutritionally balanced.

GRAINS

Many local supermarkets and natural food chains carry organic grains, such as Lundberg Farms rice. Some small health food stores may carry small amounts of grains, but, if busy, replenish their supplies quickly so they are always fresh. Ask the store when new shipments arrive and how they are packaged to make sure your baby is not exposed to potential allergens through cross-contamination.

Use caution when buying from bulk bins because the scoops may be contaminated with other products, including highly allergenic nuts. Our local store packages organic grains with throwaway scoops for each grain, while others cover the scoop with plastic and throw that out after each grain. Once you know grains are not contaminated you do not have to worry. Organic grains can also be mail ordered, but again, always check that they are not cross-contaminated with other products.

To start, my family bought our organic brown rice in sealed packages. Brown rice is the first grain to introduce, so buy it first and be familiar with how to buy the other grains such as millet, oats, barley, and quinoa.

Buying in bulk has several advantages. You will pay less, you will not run out for a while, you will have enough for the whole family, and shopping will be off your mind.

Storage of grains

Buy the freshest grains possible in quantities to last for at least one or two months (but not longer) and store them in glass mason jars with tight-fitting lids. Place the jars in dark, cool cupboards or in the refrigerator and the grains will stay fresher, longer.

If you live in a hot, humid climate where bugs get a chance to grow, we recommend that you refrigerate your grains or freeze them for at least two weeks to destroy insect larvae. Insects can chew through plastic bags, especially the thin grocery store variety, and then contaminate other food products, so always place grains in individual sealed containers.

Whole-grain breads for teething toast

Make sure that your baby's bread does not contain wheat until after the first year, as wheat is highly allergenic. Also make sure that the bread is made without honey or corn syrup, because high temperatures may not be enough to destroy the clostridium botulinum spores (bacteria) in these products. I recommend whole-grain kamut bread, which makes naturally sweet teething toast.

After one year, you can try a variety of whole-grain breads found in grocery stores, bakeries, or natural food markets. Always steer clear of highly processed refined white and brown breads. Some manufacturers add caramel coloring to turn breads brown, but it does not make them more nutritious.

Storage
Make a huge batch of teething toast (see recipe in Chapter 10) when you bring the bread home and if there is any left, freeze it immediately. In my experience, putting breads in the refrigerator dries them out. When needed, place frozen slices in the oven to make more teething toast.

Whole-grain pasta
Babies can begin eating whole-grain noodles around ten months. Pasta makes a great finger food and helps babies develop their fine motor skills. There is a great variety of whole-grain pastas available made from brown rice, kamut, or spelt in many different shapes and sizes. These noodles are full of flavor and add variety and nutrition to your baby's diet.

Surprise your baby by experimenting with different kinds of noodles and he will pick his favorites in no time. You can place uncooked pasta in glass mason jars once the package is opened to keep it fresher.

Enriched grains versus fortified grains
Enriched grains contain added nutrients found in the original grain that were lost during processing. Fortified grains add nutrients such as iron and folic acid that were not in the original grain.

Buy whole grains to make baby food, and when your child is older, only use products that contain the whole grain, not refined grains found in some cereals or teething cookies (also high in hydrogenated fats and sugars).

Fruits and Vegetables

Refrigerate produce as soon as possible, especially in warm climates. Unripe bananas, mangoes, papayas, avocados, and tomatoes may be left to ripen on the counter, while onions and potatoes may be stored in cool, dark, dry places. Short seasonal produce such as blueberries, raspberries, and strawberries can go bad very fast, so use within a day or two or freeze right away for future use.

Purchase a new vegetable scrub brush for sweet potatoes and potatoes. Wash and peel all other fruits such as peaches, apricots, pears, and apples, especially if they are nonorganic, because of huge amounts of pesticide residues in the skin. Gently wash berries and soak in a small amount of water for a few minutes to get rid of worms and dirt, but not until mushy.

Meat

If possible, purchase animal products that are "free-range organic," a method of farming where animals are allowed to roam freely and are not kept in tight quarters. Typical mass-produced store-bought poultry or meat can be full of antibiotics and growth hormones, and may have been raised in very crowded and unhealthy living conditions. For the same reasons, buy organic eggs and dairy products as well.

Producers of nonorganic eggs are now adding essential omega-3 fats to their chicken feed in the hopes of producing a healthier egg. Free-range organic eggs come from healthy chickens who were fed a good diet, and naturally contain essential fats and nutrients.

Today, organic poultry and meats are readily found at butchers, supermarkets, natural food stores, and farmer's markets. Some companies even do home deliveries. By saving money and making your own baby food, organic poultry or meat can fit into your budget.

When buying poultry or meat to feed your baby, only buy fresh meat packaged that day and puree it in the blender after cooking. Opt for lean cuts, because babies do not need that extra saturated fat.

Meat storage

Use your homemade ground turkey, chicken, or meat within one or two days or freeze immediately. If you are going to do batch cooking, start with fresh meat or poultry because you should not freeze it twice. Never refreeze thawed meats because bacteria will have a chance to grow.

FAMILY MEAL PLANNING

When you are planning the baby's menu for the week, keep the whole family in mind for your shopping trip. If squash, green beans, and broccoli are on the baby's list, everyone can enjoy them. This will help keep your food budget in line because you are not randomly buying food for different members of the family. Choose a variety of fruits and vegetables of different colors to ensure your family receives all the essential vitamins and minerals. And as an added bonus, if you have older children who are not big vegetable eaters, if they see the baby enjoying vegetables, they may insist on having them too.

chapter 5

Food Allergies and Intolerances
They Are Not the Same!

Opinions on allergies and when to introduce potentially allergic foods differ among physicians. Though this chapter follows commonly accepted practices, your physician will have a particular food introduction strategy appropriate for your child.

FOOD ALLERGIES: THE BASICS

A true food allergy involves an immune system response to a particular food and differs from food intolerance (discussed on page 57). In many cases, if a baby has an allergic reaction to a food, it will be immediate and marked, though the reaction can also occur several hours after eating the food. Allergic reactions can be gastrointestinal (cramps, diarrhea, vomiting, nausea), respiratory (wheezing, asthma, coughing, sneezing, runny nose and shortness of breath and in extreme cases difficulty breathing, or anaphylaxis), and/or on the skin (rash, eczema, hives, or swelling of the lips or around the eyes).

Anaphylaxis is a severe allergic reaction that affects all bodily systems. If not treated immediately, it can put the body into shock, cause the airway to close, and lead to death.

Asthma is a chronic inflammation of the airways and though often inherited from parents, many asthmatics also suffer from food and environmental allergies. With these children it is particularly important to introduce food slowly and follow an allergist's advice, not feeding possible allergens before one year of age.

If a reaction is observed, stop feeding your child immediately and consult your pediatrician. Giving solid food early in the day will allow you to monitor any adverse reactions that might occur before your child goes to sleep.

The potential for allergies and the need to watch for a reaction is why you should always wait at least three days between introducing new foods. Go slowly, and introduce no more than two new foods a week. Never mix new foods together unless they have both been tolerated separately. We are most vulnerable to becoming sensitized to allergens during the first two years of life. Allergies can happen as early as the first few months of a child's life.

Predispositions to allergies

Allergies do run in families, so asking relatives about this can make you aware, in advance, of potential issues. That is not to say that you should not feed your baby something your relative is allergic to. What it means is that you may want to watch for any reactions when your baby eats that food. Food allergies occur in 4 to 6 percent of infants, but children from two allergic parents have a 40 to 70 percent chance of developing an allergy.

Other than genetics, possible causes of food allergies include feeding certain solid foods too soon, giving too much of one particular food at an early age, sensitivity to a similar food, and prevalence of a particular food in the food supply (for example, rice allergy is common in Japan).

Potential allergens

Because of their potential to be allergens or their unsuitability for babies, certain foods should not be introduced until after the first year. Potentially allergenic foods include egg whites, cow's milk, peanuts, soy, tree nuts, wheat, shellfish, strawberries, chocolate, and citrus. These foods must be introduced slowly, one at a time, and with reactions recorded. Many pediatricians suggest that tree nuts and peanuts should not be given before the age of three. Given the risk of cross-contamination, bulk foods are also not suitable for baby food. Improperly cleaned bins and scoops used in a variety of products can cause contamination.

Remember that your baby will have a lifetime to try new foods. Why take a chance by introducing allergens now?

The following is a checklist to help prevent food allergies:

Introduce solids no earlier than six months
Avoid all potential allergens until after one year
Breastfeed as long as possible (six months plus)
Do not introduce milk before one year
Crushed almonds or almond milk can be introduced after one year
Do not introduce eggs until after one year
Do not introduce peanuts until after three years
Do not introduce shellfish until after three years

Sending your allergic baby to a caregiver

If your child has an allergy, advise the caregiver/staff with a note specifying what your baby can and cannot eat, or perhaps cannot even be near. If the caregiver is looking after more than one child, make sure the note and a picture of your baby are in a prominent place in the room. If your child is anaphylactic to peanuts or nuts or other foods, provide the facility with an epinephrine injection device such as an EpiPen and ensure that the caregiver knows how to use it.

Hidden ingredients

When your child starts to eat a more varied diet, allergenic and intolerant ingredients lurk everywhere. Soy sauce can contain traces of wheat,

French fries may have a coating containing wheat, salad dressings and sauces may use wheat for thickening, and dried apricots may contain a preservative known to cause allergic reactions in some children.

Food labels must be carefully read; the extra minute this takes could save an allergic child's life. If you cannot read the label or actually see it if you are at a restaurant, err on the side of caution and do not feed your child questionable food. You must also read the labels of products familiar to you. Manufacturers often change their ingredients and labeling, but not their packaging. A line of cereals that was once okay may now contain "fine print" peanut or tree nut warnings because the product is now, or always was, produced in a factory that contains nuts, thus potentially contaminating all products.

The case of the hidden allergen

The triplets were eight months old and had just started eating solids, mostly cereals. A visiting relative offered the triplets ladyfinger biscuits to teethe on and said her kids had loved them. Two of the triplets enjoyed them; however, the third broke out in a rash all over and was screaming. It didn't take long for the mother to realize that it was the egg whites in the ladyfingers when she carefully examined the package.

Living with food allergies

Sometimes reading labels is not enough. If your child has an allergy, foods once commonly on your shopping list that contain or may contain the allergen should no longer be brought into your home. Your toddler could get her hands on it or her caregiver could feed it to her by mistake. Depending on the severity of the allergy, some children may only need to be in the same room and smell the offending food or get a peck on the cheek for there to be a reaction.

Eating out

Depending on the allergy at issue, certain establishments may have to be avoided. If your child has a peanut or nut allergy, for example, do not visit Chinese, Thai, or Malaysian restaurants because of the risk of cross-contamination, as they typically use peanuts and peanut products.

Traveling with allergies

Always carry snacks that your child can eat. Do not assume that there will be food available for your child, even if you have ordered something ahead of time. If traveling by airplane, as soon as you step onto the plane, inform the staff that your child has a severe allergy, especially if there is an asthma component. Many flights have been known to sell tree nuts and ice cream, chocolate, or baked goods with nuts. Always bring wipes for your child's hands if they touch surfaces such as doors that other passengers have touched. You cannot be too careful.

COMMON FOOD ALLERGIES
Cow's milk allergy

This is, most frequently, a reaction to the milk protein casein and symptoms commonly include abdominal pains, diarrhea, and vomiting. Approximately 10 percent of babies are sensitive to milk protein to some degree, but most will outgrow it by age three. Babies and young children with this allergy can be given soy-based milk or formula. Due to the prevalence of this allergy, cow's milk is generally not recommended for children less than one year of age. If a child does not outgrow this allergy, a dairy-free diet will be necessary.

Peanut allergy

Despite its name, the peanut is not a true nut, rather it is a member of the legume family, which includes peas, kidney beans, and lentils. Not so long ago, peanut butter sandwiches were a common and easy-to-prepare lunch to take to school. Today, there is a veritable epidemic of peanut allergy, with at least 5 percent of children having it. The allergy entails a reaction to one or more of the many proteins present in peanuts, and a reaction can be caused by exposure to as little as one one-hundredth of a peanut. Some people are so sensitive that they even react to the odor of peanuts or peanut butter.

Unlike some food allergies, such as those to milk and eggs, which frequently become *less* severe as a child becomes older, peanut allergies typically do not decrease in severity over time and in fact may increase. Consult with your pediatrician about ways to reduce peanut allergies, including not introducing them prior to three years of age, and possible peanut allergy vaccines.

Given the potential severity of this allergy, which has as the common reaction anaphylaxis, cross-contamination is a significant concern. Most facilities that process peanuts also process other nuts.

Tree nut allergies

Tree nuts are "true" nuts and include cashews, brazil nuts, chestnuts, hazelnuts, almonds, pecans, walnuts, cashews, pistachios, macadamias, and pine nuts (although belonging to different plant families). Water chestnuts are not nuts.

There are so many cross-reactions that many allergists just give the diagnosis "allergic to nuts" rather than to a specific nut. Given the risk of cross-contamination, this general diagnosis is safer for your child. If a child has a peanut allergy, your doctor may suggest avoiding all nuts.

Soy allergies

Soy is a legume and a cousin of the peanut. However, an allergy to one does not mean that the child is allergic to both. If you look at processed food labels carefully, you will see how common soy is—in one of its forms it is in everything from cereal to canned soup to salad dressing to prepared meats. Many labels even read, "may contain traces of soybeans."

Egg allergies

Eggs are not recommended before one year because egg white can be highly allergenic. Some doctors or nutritionists allow egg yolks (the nonallergenic part) before nine months, but this is a cause for a concern. The egg is a whole food and, even when hard-boiled, it is almost impossible to completely separate the white from the yolk. It is possible that some children could react to the yolk.

FOOD INTOLERANCES

Food intolerances are *not* allergic reactions because there is no immune response to the allergen. However, these reactions can still be quite severe. The two most common offenders are milk and wheat.

Lactose intolerance is an inability to digest lactose, the sugar in milk, due to a deficiency of lactase, a digestive enzyme. It is sometimes confused with a milk allergy. When a lactose-intolerant person ingests milk products, reactions can include cramping and diarrhea. Unlike an allergy, lactose intolerance can be short lived and caused by a non-food-related event such a gastric virus (gastroenteritis) or a regime of antibiotics that can destroy intestinal flora, thereby not allowing one to tolerate dairy products. People with this intolerance may still be able to tolerate yogurt that contains probiotics (special bacteria that are useful for the digestive system). For some the intolerance will pass.

Gluten intolerance, like lactose intolerance, is not an allergy but can cause unpleasant symptoms. Common dietary culprits that contain the protein gluten are wheat, oats, barley, and rye. The symptoms are not unlike those for lactose intolerance: cramping, diarrhea, and possibly vomiting. The potential for this intolerance is another reason why you should not introduce grains into baby's diet before six months—their digestive systems are still developing and they may not have the enzymes needed to digest cereal grains. As with allergies, family history may have a part to play here as well.

Severe conditions of chronic gluten intolerance are called celiac disease, and people who have it must avoid all traces of gluten. This can be a very restrictive diet that does not allow the use of many grains, unlike a wheat allergy, for example, which is just restrictive against wheat. What these gluten-containing grains potentially do is irritate the small intestine's lining, which is important for the absorption of nutrients. As the intolerance interferes with digestion, consuming wheat may cause some children to become nutritionally depleted over time.

Grains that do not contain gluten are rice, millet, quinoa, and corn.

Nightshade vegetables

Nightshade vegetables (tomatoes, white potatoes, eggplant, and peppers) are hard to digest and are not recommended until after the first year. This excludes sweet potatoes and yams because they belong to another family. Similar to protein, nightshade vegetables can cause small holes to develop in a baby's immature intestinal lining. They also contain solanine (an alkaloid), which can deplete a baby's minerals, is a calcium inhibitor, and may cause diarrhea. Introduce nightshade vegetables after one year and only in small quantities.

chapter 6

Preparing Homemade Baby Food
It's Easier than You Think!

"Tell me, I'll forget. Show me, I may remember.
Involve me, and I'll understand."

—Chinese Proverb

With a little organization and a few common kitchen utensils, preparing homemade baby food is a breeze. You do not have to be a gourmet chef using special ingredients to whip up delicious meals for your baby. If green beans are on the menu, simply puree your baby's beans. Soon your little one will be enjoying foods such as lentil soups and roast chicken with potatoes—pureed of course. Our recipes are easy to follow and in no time you will be a pro.

WHY PREPARE HOMEMADE BABY FOOD?
- It tastes great! One spoonful and you and your baby will be hooked.
- You will spend less money feeding your baby.
- You will use the freshest, best-quality ingredients.
- Small-batch cooking retains nutrients.
- Natural whole foods are healthier in general.

- Baby will feel like a part of the family eating the same foods you eat.
- Baby will get used to the taste of the foods the rest of the family is eating.

ADVANTAGES OVER STORE-BOUGHT BABY FOODS

Babies need simple, natural foods so their energy can be concentrated on growing, not on digesting unnecessary ingredients. The FDA regulates commercial baby food so that it does not contain harmful additives, but these store-bought products are often mass-produced and can contain tapioca, salt, sugar, and hydrogenated or partially hydrogenated oils. Some high-quality specialty or organic baby foods are available if you need to keep a few jars on hand in case of a crisis, but overall, homemade is best.

Prepackaged foods are generally three to five times more expensive than the cost of buying bulk or raw ingredients and making baby foods at home. Remember that the cost of prepared and prepackaged foods includes the price of packaging and overhead. So, for example, a bunch of carrots and stalk of celery are relatively cheap; however, when the store cuts up these vegetables and packages them for snacks or stir-fries, they become much more expensive per unit.

Misinformation about homemade baby food

Because we live in a modern society, many people feel it is okay to let food manufacturers feed their children because manufactures supposedly produce the sterile food babies need in order to not get sick. They imagine workers in hairnets and gowns making baby food. This is a fallacy. If you follow basic kitchen safety procedures and common sense, you alone can safely feed your baby. That is what thousands of people are doing now and what generations before us did.

Do not think that if you choose to make homemade baby food you will spend your whole life in the kitchen. It is up to you to decide how much time you want to dedicate to making baby food. And for those times when you are away from home and unable to cook, there are some good organic brands of baby food available or you can package your own.

KITCHEN SAFETY

Establish a good routine early on to ensure that your kitchen is a safe place. Always follow these important safety guidelines:

Never leave the stove unattended.

Keep pot handles turned inward.

Use back stove burners only.

Keep all appliances far away from counter edges.

Keep the kettle away from the front of the counter and its cord hidden at the back.

Store knives far from Baby's reach.

Place empty pots in the sink after use.

Stay with your baby at all times during feedings.

If you need to leave the kitchen for any reason, take your child with you.

These safety practices are especially important if your child is pulling himself up to a standing position.

Kitchen hygiene and sterilization

Cleanliness is key when preparing baby food (no matter the ingredients). Thoroughly clean and sanitize all counters and work areas. Food handlers must wash their hands before and during preparation.

Sponges and dishcloths

Kitchen sponges and dishcloths are breeding grounds for bacteria and must only be used for short periods of time, less than one week. Do not use the same sponge or cloth for counters and dishes, even if they say they are antibacterial. When dishcloths are used to wash dishes, the rule is to place them in the laundry after a few days.

Use separate dishcloths to wipe up counters where meat was prepared and machine wash them as soon as possible afterward. Or use disposable paper towels for this task and just throw them away.

Cutting boards

Use a separate cutting board for preparing meats and always sanitize it well. Automatic dishwashers are great places to sanitize cutting boards. Plastic and glass cutting boards can be sanitized with antibacterial soap.

Plastic boards need to be replaced when they develop deep groves from overuse and are difficult to clean. If a wooden board is used for meats, it should be bleached at least once a month and super-sanitized with antibacterial soap after each use.

Counters

Clean counters with nontoxic sterilizing cleaners. Babies' toys end up everywhere, including on your kitchen counters, and then in their mouths, so sanitization is essential. Adults have stronger immune systems that can withstand some bacteria, but with babies, the kitchen must be sanitized after each food preparation.

Baby's equipment

Baby's high chair should be thoroughly wiped down with nontoxic sanitizers after each use. You do not want new food to be mixed with bacteria that has grown on previous meals. Babies love to pick up leftover crumbs from the high chair or on the seat and eat them. Floors must also be cleaned frequently because crawling babies will find leftover food crumbs and taste them.

Baby's bowls and utensils should be washed in the dishwasher because of the high temperatures, or alternatively scoured in the sink with the hottest water. This is why cross-contamination from dirty cloths or sponges must be avoided.

Food storage

Glass mason jars and extra baby food jars are excellent for storing baby foods. Avoid plastic containers and plastic wrap that contain harmful compounds such as polyvinyl chloride (PVC). These chemicals could mix with the food during storage or when heated in the microwave.

FOOD PREPARATION
Recommended kitchen equipment

To make homemade baby food, you will need the following kitchen equipment. Most of these items may already be in your kitchen:

- Baby food mill (grinder)
- Adult food mill (moulix)*
- Grinding bowl (suribachi or mortar and pestle to mash food)**
- Good-quality vegetable knife
- Ice cube trays or plastic baby cubes
- Blender or food processor
- Juicer
- Sturdy pots, preferably stainless steel (small to reheat foods and large for cooking grains)
- Enameled iron pots
- One fine mesh strainer and one large strainer for pasta
- Stainless steel vegetable steamer to fit inside pot
- Spatula, grater, wooden spoon, and vegetable scrub brushes

- Cutting boards
- Glass mason jars and empty baby food jars

*A moulix is a hand food mill that is a gentle way to puree baby food. They are widely available at kitchen stores.

**A suribachi is a Japanese serrated ceramic grinding bowl that is used with a wooden pestle (surikogi), commonly used to make gomashio (ground sesame seeds and salt). It is essentially a mortar and pestle and can be used to gently mash or puree baby food. Suribachis can be readily found in Asian cooking stores selling utensils and kitchen equipment. They are very quiet and easy to use and clean.

Methods of cooking

The method you use to cook your homemade baby food will depend upon the types of foods you are preparing. Below are the basic cooking methods you will find in the recipes in this book.

Steaming: best retains the nutrients of vegetables and keeps the color of green beans, broccoli.

Boiling: for potatoes, squash, and root vegetables. The skin protects the nutrients in these vegetables from being lost.

Baking: for squash, potatoes, and meat.

Stir-Fry: for vegetables, with a small amount of oil (only for babies older than one year).

Microwave Oven: works well for vegetables, although this is not the preferred choice, due to the potential for uneven cooking and temperatures.

When you prepare baby food, you can make small amounts each time and serve immediately or batch-cook enough for a month, freezing the bulk and reheating portions as necessary (see the following section on reheating foods). You can also, of course, combine both approaches for greater flexibility.

Storing and reheating baby food

Although foods will keep for a short period refrigerated, for longer storage, food should be frozen. Food may be frozen in ice cube trays for individual portions and then transferred into freezer bags labeled with the date of freezing and contents. Remove all air before sealing the bags for freezer storage. (You can suck the air out through a straw.) Cooked meat, poultry, and fish will keep in the freezer up to three months. Frozen fruit and vegetable purees and soups will keep for one to two months.

Portions: Baby food is typically prepared in portions greater than actually needed at one particular time. When feeding, always transfer a small amount of food from the container used to prepare it to the bowl your baby will eat from. Throw out all leftovers from Baby's bowl, and never stick the spoon used to feed Baby into the food you will be storing for use at a later time. Bacteria from the baby's saliva can contaminate food and harm the baby. Always cover and refrigerate unused portions.

Refrigeration: Though the optimum choice is to prepare food one day at a time, foods do keep when refrigerated. For example, grains can keep up to three days in the refrigerator but do not freeze well.

Cook fully: All animal food must be thoroughly cooked. Eggs when given should be fully cooked; yolks should not be raw or runny. Poultry should be thoroughly cooked, not pink inside.

Reheating foods: When reheating food always check the temperature. Baby's food should not feel warm or cold. What is warm for an adult is generally too hot for a baby. Test all food on the inside of your wrist a couple of times. If in doubt as to temperature, wait a couple of minutes. Exercise caution when using a microwave for heating; they often heat unevenly so that the top surface of the food may be warm, but the middle portion burning hot. Stir food well before serving.

Timesaving tips for preparing homemade baby food

- Stock up on the grains and legumes that Baby is eating.
- Keep baby food–making utensils in a central spot so you do not have to search your kitchen for them.
- Fresh is best but if there are time constraints, batch cook and possibly freeze. Pureed vegetables, fruit, soups, and beans freeze very well. Grains do not.
- Cook grains in large quantities so you have extra to mix with freshly made fruits, vegetables, or beans.
- Keep a bulletin board or white board in the kitchen and note which cooking ingredients you need to stock up on the next time you are at the store.

Special situations

It's important to keep some cereal and jars of organic baby food in your cupboard for the following special situations in which you may not be able to prepare homemade baby food.

- Mom or caregiver is ill
- Baby or other child gets sick and you cannot get out to shop
- Travel (food for vacation, in the car, etc.)
- Weather conditions such as rain or snow storms
- Restaurants (bring snacks for Baby to eat while waiting for your food)
- Special occasions such as birthdays

Good choices for organic baby food to have on hand include Earth's Best, Heinz Organic, and Gerber Organic brands.

"Our lives are not in the lap of the gods, but in the lap of our cooks."

—Lin Yutang, *The Importance of Living*

chapter 7

Welcome to Mom's Kitchen!
Starting Solid Foods

Your baby has grown so much in the first months, and now it is time to think about starting solid foods. Until now, mother's milk has been the perfect food for your child, providing optimal nutritional, immunological, and emotional benefits. Around six months, your baby's nutrient stores (such as iron and zinc) will start to become depleted. The introduction of solid foods will fill this nutritional gap and introduce your baby to new tastes and textures.

Starting your baby on solids is an exciting and special new experience for you and your child. This is when babies learn how to feed themselves and parents learn their child's favorite foods. Before you know it, your baby will be eating independently.

IS MY BABY READY?

Often parents feel pressured by friends, family, or even their culture, to start their baby on solid foods. Coupled with exhaustion, they may welcome the opportunity to stop nursing and rebuild their own energy levels. However, the key is not to rush into solids, for they may increase your child's susceptibility to allergies. Starting solid foods too early offers no nutritional advantage.

The American Academy of Pediatrics recommends that breast milk or formula be the primary food for your baby's first year, with solid foods being a dietary supplement introduced at six months of age. The latest recommendations from the World Health Organization (WHO) suggest that weaning should not occur earlier than four months of age.

Bottle-fed babies typically become interested in solids earlier than six months, around four months. Even if they are full, they may cry after feedings or start reaching for your food, so look for these signs.

Look at those choppers!

One guideline for introducing solids to a healthy baby is to begin around the time when the first teeth begin to come in. This can occur around six months of age, sometimes a little sooner. At this stage, Baby is grabbing at everything and putting it into her mouth, a developmental reflex that may be related to teething discomfort.

Other signs that your baby may be ready for solid foods include
- Baby can hold her own head up, turn her head, and sit upright without help.
- Baby is interested in food that others are eating.
- Baby opens her mouth when food is offered.
- Baby can take food from a spoon.
- Baby has doubled her birth weight.

Each baby is unique

Physiologically, your baby is now producing the enzymes necessary to digest solid foods. But babies are unique and need to be weaned accordingly. Breast milk or formula has done a great job of nourishing your baby thus far, so keep it as her main source of nutrition until she is ready to begin solids.

Babies that are not growing rapidly or gaining weight, are sleeping poorly, or appear hungry may be ready for solid foods. Babies that are not ready for solid foods will stick their tongues out and reject the food (tongue thrust reflex). This reflex helps protect your baby from choking on food.

Babies who are content, sleeping well, satisfied by their nursings, and growing well may not be interested in starting solids yet. Our own babies were so satisfied with breast milk that they did not want solids until after seven months.

Consult with your baby's pediatrician to see if your child has reached the developmental milestones to begin eating solids. For example, if your baby cannot hold her head up or control her neck, she could choke on solid food.

Taking it slow

Is your baby past seven months and still not interested in solids? Relax! Some babies are content with milk, and only when you reduce the number of feedings will they become hungry and take to solids. You still should not worry, as many doctors feel that you can exclusively breastfeed your baby for a year without any solids. Several communities in countries around the world keep to their traditions by holding off on feeding solids to their babies until they are well past nine months or even one year.

Try mixing cereal with breast milk or formula, a taste that your baby is used to. First cereals are best served runny and not thick because Baby is just pushing the cereal to the top of her mouth (gumming it) and swallowing; she is not chewing, and you do not want her to choke.

How is mom feeling?

Mom's health is also an important factor influencing when solids are started. If you are exhausted or underweight, even though you may produce enough breast milk, the quality may be low. It may not be nutritious enough to nourish Baby as she starts to crawl and becomes more active. Remember to take care of yourself, sleep well, eat well, and not overexert yourself. I was always told "rest even if for a little time while your baby is sleeping; everything else can wait."

EASY DOES IT!

Go slow—babies need to be gradually introduced to new foods to build their digestive systems. After all, they have their entire adult life to eat everything. Strong digestive tracts may help prevent many of today's illnesses. Allergists agree that many food and environmental allergies could be prevented if the process of food introduction was slower and the baby's genetics were taken into account. For infants with a family history of food allergies, a pediatrician should closely monitor solid food introduction.

You carried your baby for nine months and maybe nursed for six months more, so continue to be patient when introducing solids. First foods can be as simple as mashing a banana with the back of a fork. Take my daughter, for example, her uncle was eating a banana and my daughter kept reaching for it. We followed her lead (she was seven months) and mashed a banana with a fork and she loved it. The next day, we made her whole-grain rice cereal, and she took to it right away.

Five easy steps to weaning

1. The first six months: breast milk or formula
2. Six months plus: pureed whole-grain cereals, pureed vegetables, and fruit
3. Six months to one year: reduce milk intake by half
4. One year to eighteen months: decreases milk intake to around one quarter of food Baby eats
5. Eighteen months to two years: babies wean themselves

Baby's first tastes

The first tastes that you give your child will influence her taste patterns for the rest of her life. If your child is given a lot of natural foods such as greens and sesame seeds, she will crave these foods when her body needs calcium. If she is fed refined sugars, salt, or very oily foods, she will tend to crave these foods into adulthood. Always do your best to fill your kitchen with nutritious food. But remember to never force your baby to eat if she is not hungry.

In the first year introduce only natural tastes; leave out the herbs and spices, salt, and sugar until Baby's digestion gets stronger. Using these ingredients now could cause problems later on.

Avoid feeding your child
- salt: chips, bacon, or luncheon meats
- sugary candy (substitute pure maple syrup, brown rice syrup, natural fruit juice)
- artificial sweeteners or colors
- high-fat fried foods, fatty foods, chocolate
- foods that contain nitrates and sulfates as preservatives
- processed foods (such as cheese slices)
- honey before one year—it can contain bacterial spores (clostridium botulinium) that babies cannot detoxify in their first year

Because breast milk and formula are sweet, babies naturally prefer sweet tastes such as whole-grain cereals, butternut squash, and sweet potato. New tastes such as salty and sour are best after one year.

Cereal: The magical first food
Cereal is commonly the first food pediatricians recommend for babies at around six months of age. The whole grain, slow-cooked cereal recipes in this book retain essential nutrients, are very gentle on Baby's developing digestive system, and are creamy and velvety, resembling breast milk or formula. These cereals are the best first foods for your baby.

Past generations fed their babies—and their whole families—slow-cooked homemade porridges that both nourished and strengthened. This is almost universal worldwide, with the difference among cultures being the local grain used. For example, basmati rice is the first cereal choice in

India, millet in Africa, and rice congee in China. This book uses brown rice as the first cereal, due to its superior nutritional value, but I would not discourage someone starting with a cereal common to his or her culture.

Homemade cereals contain nutrients in their natural form (including highly absorbable forms of iron). Store-bought baby cereals are made from milled grains, a process that removes nutrients that are later added back in. These processed cereals frequently sit on store shelves for months and if not prepared carefully may resemble a paste or glue. The homemade cereals described in this book will fill your house with wonderful aromas absent from store-bought instant cereals. You will be happy when your children continue to ask for them into their toddler years.

In the past

More than thirty years ago, it was common practice to add a little store-bought cereal to your baby's bottle in the hope that her tummy would become full and she would sleep through the night. Today, pediatricians do not recommend that babies be put on any kind of solids before they are developmentally ready.

LET'S GO! THE FIRST MEAL
When?

The best times to begin are late morning (after the early morning feeding so your child won't be as fussy) or early afternoon. If you start during either of these times, you will have more than enough opportunity to monitor any of Baby's food reactions during the day. Also, choose a time when Baby is in good spirits, rather than sleepy or cranky, and when you will not be interrupted. Never introduce new foods at night in case Baby has a reaction that could be missed.

It's a good idea to start a food journal to record what your baby eats, the date it's eaten, and any reaction she has to the food. Keep this journal and use it regularly throughout the first year and into the second. It can be useful to share this information with your pediatrician if your baby has a reaction to a certain food.

Remember to introduce new foods one at a time and space them a few days apart. (See Chapter 5 for more on food allergies.)

What?

Babies need to have a diet that is mostly cooked to keep them warm, so they do not waste energy trying to digest raw or cold foods. One of the best first foods for Baby is the sweet gruel on top of brown rice cereal mixed with some breast milk or formula. It should be very thin, about the consistency of breast milk. Begin with one teaspoon for the first couple of days. Because your baby will just be pushing it to the top of her mouth and swallowing, avoid thick cereal, which could be choked on or come out the same way it went in. See Chapter 8 for recipes and cooking instructions for Baby's first cereals.

Banana is also a great first food, but make sure that it is organic and thoroughly mashed. It should easily slide off the spoon.

Once Baby begins solid foods, she will also need small amounts of water to help with digestion and to keep her properly hydrated.

Cow's milk should not be introduced before one year because it has a different protein composition than breast milk or formula, is low in iron and vitamin C, and can cause your baby to loose iron through the intestines. It is not a substitute for breast milk or formula.

How?

Nurse or bottle feed your baby a little first and then introduce some solid food on a spoon. If you do not succeed at the first meal, tomorrow is another day. Baby may take a little time adjusting to the spoon; after all, it is not the soft nipple that she is used to. You may offer the breast or bottle after the solids if she still appears hungry.

Relax!

Be happy and calm when you are feeding your baby or she may feel a little uneasy. Your baby needs time to feel comfortable and to explore and embrace the experience. If she doesn't eat everything, that's okay. Babies have small stomachs and will know when they are full; forcing those last spoonfuls often means the food will be spit out (sometimes all over you). As the baby's nurturer, you want to continue the loving bond that you have created as you begin this new feeding routine.

It may take several times before your baby is ready to accept a certain food. Be patient and continue to provide your baby with a wide variety of healthy foods. A few days can make a big difference in a baby's tastes or acceptance of food.

Babies often react to a new food by making faces, spitting the food out, playing with it, or simply refusing to eat it. Be patient; it may soon become their favorite food. Because forcing them usually makes them resist more, try these suggestions. Serve the same meal to the family (less pureed of course) and Baby (always ready to imitate) will notice this and be more willing to try her food. Try again tomorrow or next week; it may take a few times. Because babies' taste buds are unspoiled, keep the new foods healthy; it's the best time to give green vegetables such as broccoli or kale.

MEALTIME OR PLAYTIME?

Be prepared, your baby may love to stick her hands in her food or throw her bowl and spoon on the floor. To your baby it's just a game: I throw the spoon and Mom or Dad keeps picking it up. Keep your cool; the more frustrated you get, the more your baby may repeat this behavior. Give your baby some time to explore her food, but then calmly reinforce your rules (no throwing food or spitting it out onto the floor) by taking away her food.

At first, babies who are learning to eat are also learning object permanence: I throw the food but it doesn't disappear, it changes places; now it is on the floor. Babies are smart, and by the time they are self-feeding they understand that if they are hungry, they need to eat, and if they throw their food around, they will still feel hungry.

First meals can get really messy as Baby may suck the cereal off her fingers, put it in her hair, and rub the bib on her face. Don't worry; she will get used to the routine in no time. Be consistent with who feeds your baby at the beginning because you want to establish a routine that you can eventually teach to others. Siblings often like to be involved in the process.

Also keep Baby's eating area uncluttered so she can stay focused on the food in front of her. Toys, books, dolls, and stuffed animals belong in another room, not on Baby's high chair.

Self-feeding is just around the corner, so try to build good habits now. Establish meal times for each day, and schedule meals around nap times and snack times. Be prepared for a mess as your baby grabs for that spoon. For those of you who are super-neat and dislike any mess, welcome to a whole new world. You'll soon begin to laugh as you see the joy in your child's eyes as she is doing it *all by herself.*

Managing mealtime mess

- Put a plastic sheet under the baby's high chair; it is easily rolled up and thrown away after a mess.
- Put an apron over your clothes, in case the baby wants to shower you with food.
- Keep a quick change of baby clothes nearby so you can change them after the meal, rather than spreading food around the house. A little basket in the kitchen can be used to hold a couple of sleepers and outfits.

HOW MUCH FOOD IS ENOUGH?

Babies' appetites are not constant; they vary from meal to meal and from one week to the next. Sometimes babies are ravenous and demand more food, other times they are not hungry at all and end up playing with their food. As parents, we worry about these fluctuations in appetite, but it's okay unless a problem occurs at every meal. Pediatricians will reassure you that babies will not starve themselves. You should consult your doctor if your baby rejects food and milk for several feedings; in this case, she may be ill.

Growth spurts can affect a baby's appetite. I remember when my son nursed for almost twelve hours straight during a growth spurt. Babies may have insatiable appetites during these rapid periods of growth:

- The second week after birth
- At varying times over the next three months
- Between four and five months, as Baby's birth weight doubles
- At eight to ten months, especially when Baby is active and eating solids
- At one year when birth weight has tripled

Do babies need to finish everything that we give them? No. You may have been told, "Clean your plate." This certainly does not apply to babies; they are learning how to monitor their own fullness or satiety and you need to trust their signals. When they no longer want to eat, the meal is done. Force-feeding could lead to eating problems later on.

In the East

Japanese moms tell their kids to eat until they are 80 percent full; many parents from other cultures tell their children to finish everything on their plate.

Mom is Nursing Less

As your child begins solids, you may not find a big change in your feeding routine because you will still be nursing regularly. But once your baby is eating more solids and nursing less, your milk supply will decrease. Remember, the more you nurse, the more milk you produce. Nature adjusts the body perfectly. Moms who begin to nurse less rarely feel engorged because they are making less milk. If you are pumping milk for your infant, just alter your routine.

Diaper Surprises

Babies' bowel movements change once solids begin. Unlike the sweet smell from breastfed babies, after you introduce solids, there may be a more powerful odor (so powerful it may knock you over!). Bowel movements may become more solid and less frequent, and even change colors. Because Baby's digestive system is too immature to totally digest everything, poop is often colored by vegetables that are orange (squash, sweet potatoes, carrots), green (green peas, kale), and red (beets).

As Baby's food becomes more textured, you will begin to see undigested food in the diaper because Baby does not have the molars to properly chew and break the food down. Iron supplements, because they are hard for Baby to absorb and digest, may cause stools to become harder and darker. If you find anything that looks suspicious in your baby's diaper, call your pediatrician.

A surprising change

Marge got a call from her very worried husband, Marc, one evening while she was at yoga class: "Honey, I was just changing little Eric and … his poo was red! Should we take him to the emergency room?" Little did Marc know that Eric had enjoyed his first-ever serving of pureed beets for lunch.

BABY'S GROWTH

Pediatricians use growth charts to indicate how your baby is developing. These charts are averages and some babies may be smaller, which can depend on their birth weight. A baby's growth can be affected by prematurity, genetics, birth size, diet, environmental conditions, frequent illness, nutrient malabsorption, or other medical conditions. If there is a concern about your baby's weight, your pediatrician can help you determine the root cause and develop a plan of action.

Do not compare your baby to others.

Do not take other people's comments to heart; your child's growth patterns are unique.

Do speak to your pediatrician if you have any concerns.

Some parents think that their babies are too pudgy. As long as your baby is healthy and your pediatrician has no concerns, don't worry. Once your baby is moving around and using lots of energy, she will typically slim down. Remember that babies need to be fed full fats for brain development.

Now that Baby is eating more than just breast milk or formula, you need to ensure that she is receiving all the nutrients needed to grow. Your pediatrician will determine if supplements for specific nutrients are necessary. Babies usually have enough iron stores at birth for the first six months, at which time their stores start to deplete. Some pediatricians like babies to have a blood test to determine iron levels at this time.

FEEDING SCHEDULE: THE FIRST MONTH

The following is a sample feeding schedule for your baby's first month of solids. Remember that breast milk is still Baby's main source of nutrition.

The First Day

Early morning	Breast milk or formula
Mid-morning	Breast milk or formula
Lunch	Breast milk or formula and 1–2 tsp brown rice cereal gruel, very thin in texture
Mid-afternoon	Breast milk or formula
Supper	Breast milk or formula
Bedtime	Breast milk or formula

Days Two to Seven

Early morning	Breast milk or formula. If baby enjoys cereal, add to early morning meal.
Mid-morning	Breast milk or formula
Lunch	Breast milk or formula. 1 tsp brown rice cereal gruel. Gradually make thicker and increase to 1–3 tbsp if baby enjoys it.
Mid-afternoon	Breast milk or formula
Supper	Breast milk or formula
Bedtime	Breast milk or formula

Week Two

Cereal becomes thicker and can be added at supper time too.

Early morning	Breast milk or formula. If baby enjoys cereal, add to early morning meal.
Mid-morning	Breast milk or formula
Lunch	Breast milk or formula. 1–3 tbsp brown rice cereal gruel.
Mid-afternoon	Breast milk or formula
Supper	Breast milk or formula. 1–3 tbsp brown rice cereal gruel.
Bedtime	Breast milk or formula

Weeks Three and Four

Begin with millet cereal as soon as it's tolerated (it can be mixed with brown rice). The next cereal to introduce is oatmeal, followed by barley.

If Baby is doing really well with cereal, you can try the first orange vegetable puree in week four.*

Early morning	Breast milk or formula. Cereal 3–4 tbsp.
Mid-morning	Breast milk or formula
Lunch	Breast milk or formula. *First orange vegetable puree: butternut squash.
Mid-afternoon	Breast milk or formula
Supper	Breast milk or formula. Cereal 3–4 tbsp.
Bedtime	Breast milk or formula

Weeks Three and Four continued

Early morning	
Mid-morning	
Lunch	1 tsp at first; slowly increase over a couple of weeks to 3–4 tbsp.
Mid-afternoon	
Supper	
Bedtime	

"Let every father and mother realize that when their child is three years of age, they have done more than half they will ever do for its character."

—Horace Bushnell

chapter 8

Recipes for Six Months Plus

Brown rice cereal

Millet cereal

Millet and rice cereal

Oatmeal cereal

Barley cereal

Kamut flakes

Quinoa cereal

The creamy, homemade, whole-grain cereals in this chapter are packed with natural nutrients, particularly the B vitamins, iron, and fiber. Although commercially prepared cereals start off with the same grains, milling removes nutrients, which are later added back. The nutritional value of whole grains is simply superior. Babies everywhere love the homemade, sweet tasting, and velvety textured cereals made from these whole grains!

The grains used in this book's recipes are short-grain brown rice, sweet brown rice, millet, barley, oatmeal, kamut, and quinoa. I choose to use organic versions of these grains, though nonorganic versions can also be used.

GRAINS: NUTRITIONAL POWERHOUSES

Brown rice cereal is high in B vitamins, calcium, phosphorus, and iron, and is easy for Baby to digest. Millet has the highest iron content of all grains, and is rich in B vitamins, niacin, folic acid, calcium, iron, potassium, magnesium, zinc, and protein. Barley is naturally sweet and high in trace minerals. Oats are the grain with the highest protein content and a good source of iron and B vitamins, especially B_1.

Brown rice and millet make great first cereals because they both contain high amounts of absorbable iron that babies need at this stage. Babies are susceptible to iron-deficiency anemia between nine to fifteen months. They produce the enzymes needed to digest cereals at about six months.

CEREAL BASICS

The younger the baby, the longer the grains should be soaked and cooked so that they are fully digestible. Between six months and one year, use a hand food mill. For babies over one year, grains may be mashed with a potato masher, suribachi, or served soft.

Cereals may be sweetened with tiny amounts of organic rice malt or rice syrup. When your baby has teeth (usually after nine months), cereal can be mashed using a potato masher or suribachi (Japanese hand food grinder).

Here's a quick overview of how to introduce cereal to your baby. Start with brown rice cereal. Once brown rice cereal is tolerated for one to two weeks, the second and later cereals can be introduced two weeks apart. If your baby or toddler is under the weather, the basic cereals in this chapter will soothe his tummy and comfort him.

Once Baby has tried all the grains and tolerates them, you can start using mixed grain combinations at about seven months or later. Wheat is highly allergenic and is not recommended until one year. Preparations for mixed grains are the same as first cereals. I have found millet/rice, oats/rice, and oats/barley to be yummy combinations.

Six easy steps for cooking grains

Follow these instructions to cook each of the grains described in this chapter's recipes.

Wash grain in a bowl, replacing water until it becomes clear.

Soak grain (overnight for babies six to ten months, 3 to 4 hours for babies older than ten months) in a sturdy, deep pot, preferably stainless steel, as it will help retain nutrients. For babies six to nine months, use 6–8 cups of water for every cup of grain.

For babies nine to twelve months, use 4 cups of water for every cup of grain.

For babies twelve months and older use 2 to 3 cups of water for every cup of grain.

Discard and replace water after soaking and add a one-inch square piece of kombu* to the water. For babies older than one year, add a few grains of sea salt.

Boil the grain on high until a raging boil; skim top of water and let simmer. Total cooking time will vary with grain used (see recipes for cooking times). When cooking is complete, remove grain from heat, let it cool for 10 minutes, and discard kombu.

Strain the grain and save liquid for Baby to drink or to add to cereal to give it a smoother consistency when reheating after refrigeration.

Mill grain in food mill to remove bran and other indigestible fibers from the cereal.

Store cereal in glass mason jars in the refrigerator for up to three days.

*__Kombu__ is a seaweed commonly used in Asian cooking and is readily available prepackaged at health and grocery stores. It comes in dried sheets and its purpose is to increase digestibility and add minerals to the grain. Do not purchase loose seaweed as it is processed with more chemicals.

First Cereal
Brown rice cereal (begin six months plus)
Nutritional star!

- 6–8 cups filtered or spring water
- 1/3 cup organic sweet short-grain brown rice
- 2/3 cup organic short-grain brown rice

Cook for 1 1/2 hours after boiling.

Second Cereal
Millet cereal

- 6 cups filtered water
- 1 cup millet (or 3/4 cup millet and 1/4 cup sweet brown rice)

Cook for 1 hour after boiling.

Millet sometimes contains tiny stones, so the grains should be carefully checked and stones removed before washing. Cooking time is shorter, taking only about 1 hour. Millet absorbs water quickly and needs more water than rice.

Third Cereal
Millet and rice cereal

- 6–8 cups filtered or spring water
- 1/4 cup organic millet
- 1/4 cup organic sweet short-grain brown rice
- 1/2 cup organic short-grain brown rice

Cook for 1 1/2 hours after boiling.

Fourth Cereal
Oatmeal cereal

- 6–8 cups filtered water
- 1 cup rolled oats

Cook for 1 1/2 hours after boiling.

Fifth Cereal
Barley cereal

A very sweet and delicious cereal!

- 6–8 cups filtered water
- 1 cup barley

Cook for 1 1/2 hours after boiling.

Other Cereals
Kamut flakes

Kamut is packed with protein.

- 6–8 cups filtered water
- 1 cup kamut

Cook for 1 1/2 hours after boiling.

Quinoa cereal (ten months plus)

- 1 cup quinoa
- 4 cups of water

Cook for 30 minutes after boiling.

MORE ABOUT BABY'S FAVORITE GRAINS

Millet is such an important grain that it provides food for about one-third of the world's population, from China to Africa. It is an ideal substitute for people allergic to wheat and gluten. Millet is so versatile that it can be used in grain dishes, cereals, stews, vegetable patties, and soups.

Kamut is an ancient grain that has been found in the pyramids of Egypt. It is a close relative of wheat, and because it contains less gluten it can be tolerated by many people sensitive to wheat (although not for people suffering from celiac disease). Kamut is a high-energy grain, containing about 30 percent more protein than wheat. Nutritionally, it is rich in vitamins B and E, phosphorus, magnesium, zinc, and complex carbohydrates. It tastes delicious and babies love the nutty flavor. It is also great for teething toast.

Quinoa (pronounced keen-wah) is an ancient grain originating from South America. It is not a true cereal grain, but the fruit of a plant. Quinoa is a high-quality superfood because it is a complete protein containing all the essential amino acids in an easily digested form. Vegetarians could not ask for a more perfect food. Quinoa is gluten-free and rich in B vitamins, phosphorus, iron, magnesium, fiber, essential fatty acids, and complex carbohydrates. Best of all, older children love it because after cooked it looks like little flying saucers or little tails. Quick and easy to prepare, it can replace rice in any dish.

Foods for Months Seven and Eight

A t this age, babies begin to show their first signs of independence, their first food preferences, and the physical skills necessary to self-feed. It is a great time to provide your baby with a variety of foods. Many babies begin to develop the grasp reflex at about eight months of age and will start to hold food against the top of the thumb.

Baby's primary food is still milk, either breast milk or formula. But once your baby is thriving on both milk and the first cereals introduced around six months, she is ready for some new taste sensations.

PUREES AND OTHER NEW TASTES

Pureed vegetables can now be added to Baby's diet first, followed by pureed fruits (see Chapter 10 for puree recipes). Begin with soft purees that are soothing to the gums and easy on digestion. Take your time, and when Baby is ready, purees can be gradually combined and made slightly more textured. Once vegetables are tolerated, they can be mixed with cereals, the same for fruits. Teething toast is also a great new food at this stage.

At around eight months, introduce Baby to more combinations of cereal, vegetables, and fruit. Be creative! Also continue to give Baby tasty teething foods. As Baby gets more teeth, foods can be more textured to teach chewing. Babies may also begin to drink diluted organic fruit juices or baby juices (pesticide-free) at eight months, using a 3:1 water-to-juice ratio. Do not give citrus until after one year. This is a good time to introduce a training cup with a soft lid.

TEETHING

Baby's teeth are coming in! Your good-natured child may become difficult at feeding time, naptime, or bedtime when teething. Some babies cruise through this phase without much complaint while others have a rough time. Teething babies will try to put everything into their mouths, so be careful about leaving small items around the house within Baby's reach. Teething toast and other chewy foods will soothe Baby's sensitive gums (never feed your baby chewing gum). See Chapter 10 for teething toast recipes.

You can brush Baby's first teeth with a soft baby toothbrush, but continue to clean Baby's mouth with a washcloth or gauze until she has several teeth. Never put a baby to bed with a bottle of fruit juice or milk because the sugar will remain in Baby's mouth, causing tooth decay. Healthy gums and primary teeth are the foundation for permanent teeth. Most children have their complete set of twenty primary teeth by three years of age.

FRUIT JUICES

Diluted, non-citrus fruit juices can be introduced at eight months of age and served in a sippy cup. Buy juices that are 100 percent pure, not cocktail or other juices containing sugar. Juices must be pasteurized to prevent possible bacterial contamination. Preferred juices are natural peach, pear, and apricot. If making homemade carrot juice, only use organic carrots because nonorganic varieties may contain undesirable contaminants from the soil. Orange and apple juices served by themselves may be too acidic for babies' tummies.

Juices contain vitamins and minerals, but lack the beneficial fiber present in whole fruits. Fruit is best served in its natural state because it has the most nutrients. Homemade organic juices are the next best choice, but should be served immediately, not refrigerated. All juices need to be diluted to 3 parts water to 1 part juice until Baby is eleven months.

Be careful not to give your baby too much juice. Recent nutritional studies suggest that excessive juice consumption among babies and toddlers can contribute to the development of obesity at an early age. The American Academy of Pediatrics suggests no more than 3/4 cup (about 6 ounces) of juice daily, and some pediatricians recommend no juice at all for babies and young toddlers. Juice is a very concentrated source of sugar (fructose) and may cause gas or diarrhea if consumed in excess. It is not a substitute for breast milk or formula. Too much juice can fill your child up and prevent her from getting the calories and nutrients she needs. Water is more effective than juice for keeping your baby properly hydrated.

> Serve Baby's juice and other beverages at room temperature (not cold) because Baby's digestive system requires warmth, not coolness.

GOODNESS FROM THE SEA

People from Asian countries have been enjoying a wide variety of sea vegetables for thousands of years. For those of us who love Japanese food, you are already eating these wonderful vegetables (the green seaweed wrapped around sushi rolls called *nori,* as well as the *wakame* that is in miso soup). We can look to the sea for nutrition, as sea vegetables are high in trace minerals such as iodine, B vitamins, calcium, and magnesium.

In North America, sea vegetables are commonly used by food manufacturers as thickeners and stablilizers in products such as ice cream, rather than for nutrition. However, many people value sea vegetables for their super-nutritional qualities, and I include them in some of the cereal and bean recipes in this book. My first choice is kombu, a seaweed that adds natural salt, vitamins, and minerals to cereals and makes beans more digestible by absorbing their gas-causing substances.

Other varieties of seaweed include wakame, dulse, arame, kelp, nori, and hijiki (hiziki). Include these amazing foods in your baby's diet, but only in small amounts to keep the minerals in balance. Choose high-quality sources that are not sprayed or contaminated with pesticides or fungicides. Refer to the Website resource section for more information.

Once your baby is familiar with the subtle tastes from sea vegetables, it will be easy to continue using them later. Sea vegetables eaten in combination with fish provide a great source of vitamin B_{12} and are recommended over dairy products, eggs, and meat.

FOOD INTRODUCTION SUMMARY (WHAT TO FEED AND WHEN)

AGE	Birth to 6 months	6 to 9 months
FOODS	Breast milk or formula	Pureed whole-grain cereals cooked with a tiny piece of kombu, no salt, and a tiny amount of organic brown rice malt or syrup, vegetables, fruit.
GENERAL		Always use organic foods if possible. Begin with soft purees that are soothing to the gums and easy on digestion. As Baby gets more teeth, foods can be more textured to teach him how to chew. A training cup (soft lid) can be introduced.

Food Introduction Summary *continued*

SPECIFIC MONTHS		**6 months**—breast milk or formula is still the focus of baby's diet. Baby should be fed milk first and solids second. First food—whole-grain cereals. Order of introduction: rice, millet, oats, and barley. Do not introduce wheat until after 1 year. Feed Baby 1 tsp of cereal at a time mixed with breast milk or formula. Gradually increase cereal amount until Baby is full. **7 months**—pureed vegetables may be added to baby's diet first, and then pureed fruits. Once vegetables are tolerated, they may be mixed with cereals, the same for fruits. Teething toast. **8 months**—introduce baby to more combinations of cereal, vegetables, and fruit. Be creative. Teething foods. Babies may begin to drink diluted organic fruit juices or baby juices, pesticide free, 3:1 water-to-juice ratio. Do not give citrus until after 1 year. **9 months**—All vegetables may be introduced, spinach, turnips. Cereals, fruits, and vegetables become more textured and are offered in new combinations.

chapter 10

Recipes for Months Seven and Eight

Mom's kitchen is now cooking up chunkier meals. Babies may not have all their teeth, but their gums can handle it!

WHAT'S NEW ON THE MENU?

Teething foods
Vegetable purees
First orange purees—butternut squash, carrots, sweet potato
First green purees—peas, green beans
Second vegetable purees—broccoli, cauliflower, leafy greens, beet, and many more . . .
Fruit purees—apple, pear, banana . . .
Cereals with vegetables and fruit

TEETHING FOODS

Your baby will want to put everything into his mouth when he is teething. These tasty and nutritious foods will help soothe those tender gums.

Teething toast / zwieback (seven months plus)

Zwieback is of German origin and translates as "twice baked." It is a bread that is slowly toasted in the oven and makes a great teething toast and toddler snack, as it is easily digested. Babies love the sweet taste!

• 6 slices of unsalted whole-grain yeast-free bread

Preheat *oven to 250°F.*

Slice *bread into quarters.*

Lay *bread on clean oven racks.*

Bake *at this low temperature for about 1 hour, turning once until golden brown.*

Store *in a sealed container or a paper bag for up to 2 weeks.*

Tasty teethers (eight months plus)

• Teething toast (zwieback)
• Large whole carrot from freezer—cut off sharp end (do not use once teeth erupt)
• Hard bagel (not wheat)
• Rice cakes or puffed cereals
• Natural teething cookies (not wheat), sweetened with pure fruit juice (until teeth come in)
• Whole-grain toast (not wheat)
• Cold pureed peaches

VEGETABLES

By seven to eight months of age, your baby is ready to enjoy the delicious flavors of vegetables. Smoothness is the key, and cooking them in minimal amounts of water will help to retain nutrients. Vegetables can be pureed in a food mill or blender (especially green beans and peas). Puree potato or sweet potato using a hand blender or food mill, because a regular blender will make them gooey.

Vegetables that are too thick will be difficult for Baby to swallow, so make sure to monitor the consistency closely. Simply add more liquid (breast milk, formula, or water) a little at a time until you reach the desired consistency.

The first pureed vegetables from Mom's diner such as carrot and sweet potato are sweet and mild. Second vegetables such as broccoli are stronger tasting and are served with more texture. Vegetables are best served alone or mixed with cereals, but not with fruits (except apples). Fruits should be introduced after vegetables, as Baby will receive enough sweetness from the orange vegetables first. This prevents Baby from getting a sweet tooth and losing interest in vegetables.

Babies love finger food. After eight months, Baby can be served small, melt-in-the-mouth cooked squash squares and later, when teeth start to come in, little soft broccoli pieces.

Choose carefully

Feeding your baby corn (highly allergenic) and nightshade vegetables (white potatoes, tomatoes, eggplants, and peppers) before one year is not recommended. Root vegetables such as carrots readily absorb chemical fertilizers, so always choose the organic varieties of these foods.

Give the chef a break!

We all know that dinnertime can be a busy time in many households; preparing some of baby's food in bulk may save the day. Serve the same vegetables for the family that you are cooking for Baby (of course in a less pureed form) to make it easy. Most recipes produce extra food for freezing.

Orange Vegetable Purees (Seven Months Plus)

Babies enjoy sweet tastes for first foods because they resemble breast milk. Orange vegetables make great first choices.

Butternut squash

Squash is tasty, high in fiber and complex carbs, and a great source of vitamin A ... a wining combination!

• 3–5 cups of butternut squash, peeled and cubed

Cook *squash in a steamer or double boiler; or you can use a small saucepan with enough boiling water to just cover squash.*

Simmer *covered until soft for about 15 minutes.*

Puree *using a small amount of the cooking liquid. For older babies, mash with a fork or use a suribachi.*

Carrots

• 1–2 cups of organic carrots, peeled and diced

Cook *according to the directions for the first orange vegetable puree (squash).*

Try this recipe substituting another root vegetable such as parsnip. You can then make a tasty combination, carrot-parsnip puree (once both are tolerated).

When Baby has an upset tummy, hold off on carrots because they can make indigestion worse or cause diarrhea.

Sweet potato puree

Sweet potatoes are nutritional champions, high in vitamins A, C, and beta-carotene.

• 3–5 small sweet potatoes, peeled and diced

Place *sweet potatoes in a small saucepan and add enough boiling water to completely cover.*

Cook *covered until soft for about 15 minutes.*

Puree *using a hand blender or food mill (avoid using a regular blender because the potato will become gooey instead of creamy).*

You may use some cooking water, breast milk, or formula to get the desired consistency.

> Orange baby? Don't worry—you may have given him too many orange vegetables; the extra beta-carotene may turn his skin a little orange. Just cut back on these foods and this harmless condition will go away.

GREEN VEGGIE PUREES (EIGHT MONTHS PLUS)
Peas or green bean puree

Peas are sweet, delicious, always a baby favorite, and bursting with vitamin C, beta-carotene, fiber, and zinc.

• 3–5 cups of frozen or fresh peas or cut green beans, ends trimmed

Cook *in a small saucepan with a small amount of water covering the peas or beans halfway.*

Simmer *with lid on for about 3 minutes until soft, but keeping the bright green color.*

Puree *using a small amount of the cooking water for a smooth puree.*

Second Veggie Purees (eight months plus)

Baby is ready for stronger tastes!

Broccoli puree

Broccoli has a strong, distinct flavor and if your baby turns his nose up, mix with some sweet potato.

• 2 cups of broccoli florets (you may substitute cauliflower), ends trimmed

Wash *broccoli well, soak in water for a few minutes, and drain.*

Place *broccoli in a small saucepan and add enough boiling water to cover broccoli halfway.*

Boil *with lid on and reduce heat to medium for a few minutes until tender, but still bright green; discard water.*

Puree *using a small amount of breast milk or formula (the cooking water from gassy vegetables such as broccoli or cauliflower can make Baby gassy, so do not use it for the puree).*

Cauliflower puree

Follow the same recipe as the broccoli puree above.

Leafy greens

Leafy greens like these are high in calcium, beta-carotene, and vitamin C.

• 3 cups of chopped bok choy (easiest to puree), washed

Steam *bok choy in a steamer basket until soft, but still retaining its green color.*

Puree *and add a little fresh water or mother's milk to get the desired texture.*

If Baby enjoys bok choy, try kale and collards. Greens mix well with pureed orange vegetables and boost their calcium.

Beet puree

• 2 medium or 1 large beet, washed, peeled, with ends cut off and diced

Place *beets in a small pot and add enough water to just cover the beets.*

Cook *on high until boiling, cover, and simmer for about 10 minutes until fork soft.*

Puree, *adding a little cooking water if necessary for smoothness.*

Don't worry, beets may turn Baby's pee and poo red because he can't digest it all yet.

Give Me Doubles!

Once all vegetables are tolerated, try these baby-tasted and approved combinations. Then create your own.

• Broccoli and carrot puree
• Carrot and parsnip puree
• Kale and squash puree
• Zucchini and green bean puree
• Squash, onions, and kale puree
• Green beans and sweet potato puree
• Butternut squash and corn puree (only after one year)

Broccoli and carrot puree

Broccoli is packed with calcium for strong bones and antioxidants, vitamin C, and beta-carotene for immunity, eyes, and skin.

- 1 cup of broccoli florets, trimmed
- 1 medium carrot, washed, peeled, and diced

Wash *broccoli well, soak in water for a few minutes, and drain.*

Place *broccoli in a small saucepan and add enough boiling water to cover broccoli halfway.*

Boil *with lid on and reduce heat to medium for a few minutes until tender, but still bright green; discard water.*

Cook *carrot separately by steaming or in a saucepan with a small amount of water.*

Puree *broccoli and carrots lightly.*

Broccoli and sweet potato puree

- 1/2 cup of broccoli florets, trimmed
- 1/2 cup sweet potato, peeled and diced

Wash *broccoli well, soak in water for a few minutes, and drain.*

Place *sweet potato in a saucepan and add enough boiling water to completely cover and bring to a boil.*

Simmer *for 5 minutes.*

Add *broccoli and continue to cook for another 8–10 minutes.*

Puree *until smooth.*

Zucchini and carrot puree

- 2 small zucchini, washed, peeled, with ends cut off and diced
- 1 large carrot, washed, peeled, and diced

Place zucchini and carrots in a saucepan and add enough water to cover.

Boil with lid on and then simmer for about 10–12 minutes until soft.

Puree until velvety smooth, adding a little cooking water if needed.

Kale and squash puree

- 2 cups of chopped kale, washed
- 2 cups of squash, washed, peeled, and diced

Steam kale (see leafy greens recipe on page 104).

Cook squash in a steamer or double boiler. If you have neither, boil squash in a saucepan with enough water to cover the amount of squash used.

Simmer squash covered until soft, for about 15 minutes.

Add kale to the squash.

Puree using a small amount of the cooking water. For older babies, mash with a fork.

MAKE MINE A TRIPLE, PLEASE!

The sweet taste of root vegetables such as parsnips and turnips may surprise you when cooked with root vegetables such as carrots, sweet potatoes, or beets. Your baby will devour them and they will become a new staple on your shopping list.

Remember that root vegetables grow deep in the ground, absorbing what is in the soil (including pesticides), so try to buy this produce organic.

Autumn veggies

- 1 carrot, washed, peeled, and diced
- 1/2 beet washed, peeled, with ends cut off and diced
- 1/4 turnip washed, peeled, and diced

Place *ingredients into a saucepan and add enough water to cover.*

Boil *and then simmer covered for about 10–12 minutes.*

Puree *with a little liquid.*

Root vegetable trio

- 2 sweet potatoes, peeled and diced
- 3 carrots washed, peeled and diced
- 1 parsnip washed, peeled and diced

Place *ingredients into a saucepan and add enough water to cover.*

Boil *and then simmer for 15–20 minutes.*

Puree *with a little liquid.*

Sweet orange veggies

- 2 cups of butternut squash, peeled and cubed
- 1 large carrot, peeled and diced
- 1 medium sweet potato, peeled and diced

Place *all three vegetables in a medium saucepan and cover with water.*

Boil *and then simmer covered for 15–20 minutes until soft.*

Puree *with a little liquid; leave some texture.*

Combines well with millet cereal.

Cauliflower, carrot, and bok choy

• 1/2 cup of cauliflower florets, trimmed
• 1/4 cup of carrot, peeled and diced
• 1/3 cup of bok choy, washed

Wash cauliflower well, soak in water for a few minutes, and drain.

Steam carrot for 2 minutes, then add cauliflower and cook until soft, but not mushy.

Remove both from steamer basket.

Steam bok choy for a couple of minutes, but keep green.

Puree together.

More triple combinations for advanced eaters

• Zucchini, carrots, and sweet potato
• Green peas, carrots, and broccoli
• Green peas, sweet potato, and kale
• Green beans, kale, and zucchini
• Squash, onions, and kale
• Butternut squash, kale, and corn (only after one year)

FRUITS

Pass the fruit bowl! Fruits can be introduced at around eight months, after cereal and vegetables. Babies love the juicy tastes of their first cooked fruits such as apples, pears, peaches, and apricots. Fruit that is just ripe and very sweet makes the best purees. The sweet taste of banana is always a hit as a first fruit—so easy to prepare, just mash with a fork!

Citrus fruits and strawberries are best left until after one year as they are allergenic. Raw fruits such as apples and pears are best left until nine months of age because they may contain spores of clostridium botulinum (causing food poisoning).

Too much fruit can cause diarrhea, so go easy on the amount you give your baby. Babies already get lots of sweetness from breast milk and sweet orange vegetables such as squash.

Fruit tips
- Fruits in season make the sweetest purees.
- To thicken fruit puree, add a little cooked cereal or mashed ripe banana.
- Fruits are best digested at snack and dessert time, when they are given by themselves.

FIRST FRUIT PUREES
Serve as a dessert after cereals and vegetables.

Applesauce (seven months plus)
The saying "An apple a day keeps the doctor away" is true, as this fruit is high in vitamin C and fiber.

- 5 sweet organic apples (Macintosh, yellow delicious, red delicious, or royal gala) washed, peeled, cored, and diced

Place *in a heavy saucepan with water covering the lower 1/4 of the apples.*

Boil *then cover and let simmer for about 10–15 minutes or until soft.*

Puree *with a little of cooking water.*

Apple-pear sauce (seven months plus)

Bursting with juicy flavors, pears are high in vitamin C and beta-carotene.

• 3 apples washed, peeled, cored, and diced
• 3 pears washed, peeled, cored, and diced

Place *in a heavy saucepan with water covering the fruit a little less than halfway.*

Boil *and then simmer covered for about 10–15 minutes or until soft.*

Puree *with a little bit of cooking water.*

Peach or apricot puree (eight months plus)

• 4 ripe peaches or 5 apricots

Cook *as in the applesauce recipe.*

Tip: how to peel a fresh peach or nectarine
Cut a light cross on the peach or nectarine and plunge into boiling water for a minute. Cool for 1 minute, peel, cut in half, throw out the pit, and puree as desired.

Dried apricot puree (eight months plus)

Choose unsulfured apricots (see Chapter 5)

• 1 cup of organic dried apricots, washed
• 2 cups of natural apple juice or baby apple juice

Place *in a heavy saucepan with water, covering the fruit a little less than halfway.*

Boil, *cover, and simmer for about 10 minutes.*

Puree *with some cooking liquid.*

MASH 'EM UP! NO COOKING REQUIRED (EIGHT MONTHS PLUS) 🌿
Banana puree

• 1 ripe organic banana

Mash *banana with a fork. You may add some milk to thin the mixture.*

"Baby guacamole" avocado puree

Avocados are high in good fats, and antioxidant vitamins A, C, and E. Babies love their creamy texture; they are delicious combined with bananas and peaches.

Cut *an avocado in half, remove the pit, scoop out the flesh, and mash with a fork or in a suribachi. You may add some breast milk or formula. For older babies (eight months plus) make it a little chunkier.*

SECOND FRUIT PUREES 🌿

These purees are a little chunkier. They also taste great blended with yogurt for babies nine months and older.

Apple-pear (same recipe as page 110, but chunkier)

• 3 apples washed, peeled, cored, and diced
• 3 pears washed, peeled, cored, and diced

Place *fruit into a heavy saucepan with water, covering the fruit a little less than halfway.*

Boil, *cover, and simmer for about 10–15 minutes or until soft.*

Puree *with a little cooking water, but leave some chunks.*

Apricot-banana

- 1 ripe banana mashed with a fork
- 1/2 cup of freshly cooked and pureed peaches or apricots

Mix *banana and peaches or apricots together in a mixing bowl.*

Serve *quickly before banana turns brown.*

KEEP ON MASHING!
Avocado-banana

- 1/2 avocado
- 1 banana

Cut *avocado in half, remove the pit, scoop out the flesh, and mash with a fork.*

Mash *banana with a fork.*

Combine *together in a bowl.*

Banana–mango puree

- 1 banana mashed with a fork
- 1/2 cup mango, washed, peeled, and diced

Mix *fruit together in a mixing bowl.*

MORE COOKED FRUIT DELIGHTS
Peach-apple-mango

- 1 ripe peach washed, peeled, cored, and diced
- 1 apple washed, peeled, cored, and diced
- 1 cup mango washed, peeled, cored, and diced

Cook for 10 minutes until all fruit is soft.

Puree a little, still leaving it chunky for older babies.

Blueberry-peach-mango (eight months plus)

- 1/4 cup fresh blueberries, washed
- 1 small peach, washed, peeled, and diced
- 1/4 cup mango, washed, peeled, and diced

Boil 2–3 tablespoons of water in a saucepan, add peach and mango, cover and simmer for 5 minutes.

Add blueberries and simmer for 4–5 minutes until soft.

Puree all fruits.

If desired, thicken with a little baby rice cereal.

Prune-apple or pear puree

If your baby really needs to go but can't, this natural high-fiber recipe will get things moving!

- 5 pitted prunes
- 2 apples or ripe pears washed, peeled, cored, and diced

Place in a heavy saucepan with water covering the fruit a little less than halfway.

Boil, cover, and simmer for about 10 minutes.

Remove outer skin of prunes.

Puree with some cooking liquid.

Apricot-pear-apple puree

- 1 apple washed, peeled, cored, and diced
- 1 pear washed, peeled, cored, and diced
- 5 dried apricots

Place apples and pears in a heavy saucepan with water covering the fruit a little less than halfway.

Boil, cover, and simmer for about 10 minutes.

Mix apple, pear, and apricots together in mixing bowl.

Puree with some cooking liquid.

Peachy-plum puree

- 1 ripe peach (nectarine) washed, peeled, cored, and diced
- 2 ripe plums washed, peeled, cored, and diced

Place peaches and plums in a heavy saucepan with water covering the fruit a little less than halfway.

Boil, cover, and simmer for about 7 minutes

Puree with some cooking liquid.

Remove the skins.

Puree all of them.

A summer taste sensation!

Cherry blush

Cherries are high in vitamin C for immunity and help with constipation.

- 1/2 cup cherries, washed, peeled, and pitted

• 1 peach or 2 apricots, peeled, and diced

Place *fruit in a saucepan, add a little water, and boil.*

Simmer *covered for 8 minutes.*

Natural energizer!

Apricot-mango tango

Dried apricots are rich in iron, beta-carotene, and fiber.

• 1 cup washed organic dried apricots
• 2 cups natural apple juice or baby apple juice
• 1 cup mango washed, peeled, cored, and diced

Boil *juice, apricots, and mango in a saucepan.*

Cover *and simmer for about 10 minutes.*

Mash *or puree with some cooking liquid. Leave some chunks for older babies.*

Banana-apricot-mango

• 1 small banana peeled
• 1/2 cup of chopped dried apricots, washed
• 1/2 cup of mango, washed, peeled, and diced

Boil *apricots and mango in a saucepan.*

Simmer *covered for 8–10 minutes until soft.*

Puree *banana with a fork in a mixing bowl, and add apricot-mango mixture.*

Baby fruit compote

- 1/4 cup dried apricots, washed and chopped
- 1/3 cup dried pitted prunes, chopped
- 2 apples, washed, peeled, cored, and diced
- 1 ripe pear, washed, peeled, cored, and diced
- 1 tablespoon of baby apple juice or water

Place all ingredients in a small saucepan and add 1 tablespoon of water or baby apple juice.

Boil, cover, and simmer for 20–25 minutes, stirring occasionally. If juices run low, add a little water.

Puree.

Mix Them up! Cereals and Vegetables (eight months plus)

Keep extra cooked cereal on hand and mix it with vegetables to make these wonderful combinations. Baby may enjoy stronger-tasting vegetables such as broccoli when they are sweetened with a little cereal.

Cereals	Vegetables
Millet	Squash, sweet potato and kale carrots, broccoli and sweet potato
Brown rice	Green peas, green beans, carrots and potato (12 months +), green beans (peas) and potato (12 months +)

continued from page 117

Cereals	Vegetables
Oatmeal	Carrots and green peas Sweet potato
Barley	Zucchini and carrots

Simply blend cooked vegetables with cereals for the following recipes. If you need further cooking instructions, turn to the vegetable or cereal recipes given earlier. Add breast milk or formula to get the desired consistency.

Brown rice and peas

- 1 cup of cooked brown rice
- 1 cup of cooked green peas or green beans

Combine *the cooked brown rice cereal and cooked green peas or green beans with breast milk or formula, and puree until smooth.*

Sweet 'n creamy!

Millet with squash

- 1 cup cooked millet cereal
- 1 cup of cooked butternut squash

Combine *the millet cereal and squash with breast milk or formula, and puree until smooth. After age eight months, you may substitute carrots for squash.*

Oatmeal, sweet potato, and apples

- 1 cup of cooked oatmeal
- 1 cup of cooked apples
- 1/2 cup cooked sweet potato

Combine *all of the ingredients and puree until desired consistency.*

Millet, sweet potato, and kale

- 1 cup of cooked millet

- 1 cup of cooked sweet potato
- 1/4 cup steamed kale

Combine *ingredients and puree with 1 tablespoon of breast milk or formula until smooth.*

Surprise your baby and come up with more tasty combos of your own!

CEREAL AND FRUIT PUREES (EIGHT MONTHS PLUS)

These purees make great desserts! Save time by having cooked grains in the fridge ready to be mixed with Baby's favorite fruit. Cereals combine best with apples, though other fruits can be given as well. Here are some baby-tested and approved combos.

Cereals	Fruit
Brown rice	Applesauce, dates or raisins, pear-apple
Oatmeal	Banana, peaches, banana, plums
Millet	Bananas, dates, apricot, peach

Apples 'n rice

- 1 cup of homemade brown rice cereal, cooked

- 2 tablespoons of applesauce

Mix brown rice cereal with applesauce and heat on low until warm. After it is warmed you may also add some of the rice milk that was saved when the original brown rice was cooked or mother's milk.

Naturally sweet, high in iron and B vitamins!

Sweet brown rice

- 1 cup of cooked homemade brown rice cereal
- 1 tablespoon of chopped dates or raisins
- 1/2 teaspoon maple syrup

Mix cereal, raisins, or dates with desired milk and heat on low until warm.

A baby favorite!

Oatmeal and bananas

Oats are rich in B vitamins, calcium, iron, magnesium, and potassium.

- 1 cup of cooked oatmeal
- 1/2 ripe banana

Mash banana with a fork and heat together with oatmeal in a pot. A small amount of mother's milk may be added at the end for desired consistency.

Cook on low heat to warm.

Lip-smacking combination!

Banana, plum, and brown rice cereal

- 1 ripe banana mashed
- 1 cup of cooked brown rice cereal

- 1–2 ripe pureed plums

Heat *cereal, banana, and plums at low temperature till warm. A small amount of milk or water may be added for desired consistency.*

Yummy!

Millet, bananas, and dates

Dates are high in iron, B-complex vitamins, and minerals.

- 1 cup of cooked millet cereal
- 1/2 ripe banana mashed
- 1 tablespoon of chopped dates or dried apricots

Mix *millet, banana, and dates together in a pot and heat on low till warm.*

chapter 11

Foods for Months
Nine to Twelve

aby is at an age of curiosity and exploration, and is now learning to feed herself. This is a time when her senses are heightened. She will want to touch, smell, and taste (and sometimes spit out) her food. Encourage her, but be prepared for the mess and *take cover*.

ALL BY MYSELF

It's beautiful watching your baby explore, but can you handle this in your kitchen along with the mess when she takes the spoon? Relax—throw out that neat freak attitude and embrace your baby's new stage. There's now a little artist in your kitchen decorating your walls and floors, herself, and sometimes you. Your baby will soon discover that if she wastes her food, she will be hungry. Your reward is an independent self-feeder.

Babies can now pick up food between their thumb and forefinger (using the pincer grasp). This is Baby's first step toward a lifetime of self-feeding. Finger foods are perfect at this stage because Baby will want to pick up everything. Serve small soft finger foods such as cooked broccoli florets and wedges of ripe fruit such as peaches or pears. Remove the pits or seeds from all foods so Baby does not choke.

At first, your child will need help feeding herself because her fine motor skills and coordination are still developing. It's not an easy task for babies to fill the spoon and get it to their mouths. It helps to feed baby foods that will stick to her spoon, such as cereal, pureed soup, and vegetables. With our kids, we played a game; we each had a spoon and they did one mouthful, and we did the next until they became proficient. Be patient; your baby will eventually be less frustrated and full, and she will be a pro in no time.

> *Tip:* Keep an extra change of clothes for your baby, and washcloths and an apron for you, in a basket nearby.

TEXTURED FOODS ARE IN

As Baby gets more teeth, foods should become more textured. Some babies love to test their new chompers, and relish the new textures. Others may resist at first, so go slowly and keep Baby's foods a little smoother until she takes to them. Babies are learning to chew and even those that have a few teeth can use their gums to help break down the food before swallowing.

Babies can continue enjoying all the delicious foods from the previous two stages, but with more texture. New finger foods such as small cooked carrots or soft fruits such as pears are great for Baby to practice her latest skills. Once your baby handles these, you may try thinly grated vegetables. Most foods are still served cooked and warm, as this is better for Baby's digestion. Cold foods are not beneficial at this age, except to provide some relief from teething pain.

WHAT'S NEW ON THE MENU?

Yogurt (natural with probiotics) provides your baby with balanced energy, calcium, and B vitamins. Introduce yogurt when your baby is around nine months. Combine it with fresh fruit purees for a tasty mix of tart and sweet flavors.

At around ten months, if Baby is ready, new plant-based proteins (legumes, soy) or animal-based proteins (organic chicken and turkey) can be given. The best legumes are steamed organic tofu (soy), adzuki beans, split mung beans, chickpeas, and lentils.

Meat can be introduced after the first year, but if you choose red meat, use very small quantities. Fish or organic poultry are healthier choices. Babies starting proteins should not be served too many at one time, because they need to get used to digesting each type of protein.

Babies love tahini, a delicious dip made from ground sesame seeds (a potential allergen) commonly used in Middle Eastern foods. Tahini can be introduced around ten months. It is high in calcium and contains healthy fats and considerable amounts of protein, calcium, and vitamins B and E.

Because all of these foods are new to your baby, they do not need to be flavored with herbs, spices, salt, or sugar. Your baby has a sensitive palate and digestive system and natural tastes are always best. Keep foods simple; gourmet food is not what your baby needs.

ESTABLISHING A FEEDING SCHEDULE

Babies thrive on a consistent feeding schedule because their digestive systems will begin to expect food at certain times, thus making digestion easier. Most babies eat three small meals and two snacks each day. Baby's diet should include at least 3–4 servings of fruits and vegetables and 3–4 servings of carbohydrates per day. Babies eating either plant- or meat-based protein can have up to 2 servings of vegetable protein or 1 serving of meat daily.

Provide your child with two snacks a day, one mid-morning and the other mid-afternoon. Fruits and vegetables are best because they are healthy, provide good concentrated energy, and are high in fiber so they satisfy your baby until the next meal. Snacks can be a great way to quickly pack in some extra nutrients, and your baby does not need to sit still in a high chair for very long. During growth spurts, you may have to add more snacks so Baby gets all she needs to grow.

Typical babies at this age drink 16–24 ounces of milk daily. Some babies dive into solids and drink less milk, while others resist solids and only want to drink. Too much liquid will fill them up, leaving little room for food. Some may carry this behavior into their second year and are called "milk babies" because they get their calories from milk. Milk plays a vital role in nourishing your child, but if it replaces solids, it could lead to deficiencies in nutrients such as iron. Water is also necessary now that Baby is eating solids. At least 6 ounces of water per day should be included in her meals by the time she is one.

Be careful not to give your baby too much juice. If given the chance, some babies will prefer juice to eating. Too much juice means too much sugar, and although natural, it can cause diarrhea or less weight gain. Serve no more than 6 ounces per day in the first two years. Doctors have shown that babies become hungrier once they decrease their juice intake. (See the section on juice in Chapter 9.)

As your baby's caregiver, be observant of how she looks, feels, and behaves, and be ready to adjust her food accordingly. For instance, if your baby has freezing cold hands, she may need some warming soup; if she wakes up tired, some energizing food will help.

BABY IS NOT READY FOR THESE FOODS YET

- Garlic is too strong for babies, unless used in tiny amounts therapeutically to treat colds (same as onion). Small amounts of onion are great in soups.

- Hold the salt until Baby is one year old and then only use tiny amounts. Excess salt is hard on the kidneys.
- Do not use margarine, shortening, hydrogenated, or poor-quality oils. Use organic unrefined cold-pressed oils, such as olive, sesame, safflower, or sunflower. Babies need omega-3 and omega-6 fats. Flaxseed and oil are superior plant-based sources of essential fatty acids. Flax oil should not be heated to prevent loss of nutrients.
- Feed babies mostly cooked food. Because raw food is harder to digest and can make the stomach cold, serve in small amounts.
- Serve food and drinks at room temperature or warm, not cold.
- Avoid spices and condiments in the first year, including ketchup and mustard.
- Some babies are not ready for new proteins found in plant or animal products.
- Fried foods are too hard for Baby to digest in the first year.
- Never give your baby unpasteurized soft cheeses such as brie or camembert in the first year because of the chance of listeria infection.

Molly loves her bottle

Since beginning solids, my eight-month-old daughter Molly was more interested in her formula than eating. We decided to give her a bottle when she cried for it. After a routine checkup, our pediatrician called to say that her iron was low and she would have to be supplemented. She was also taken off her present formula and put onto an iron-fortified one for a short period. Our doctor said that babies may not always show the typical signs of iron deficiency such as lethargy and loss of appetite.

Careful, Baby Could Choke

As your child is now self-feeding and eating a varied diet, be very careful with the foods you serve, especially finger foods. Stay with your child when she is eating because any food could potentially be a choking hazard. Feed your child in her high chair and do not let her run around with food in her hands or mouth.

If your child does choke, always take her to the doctor for an examination because small pieces of food can lodge in her respiratory tract, causing it to swell and possibly closing the air passage after a few days.

Hazardous foods until age three include nuts, hot dogs, grapes, popcorn, seeds (sunflower, pumpkin), raw carrots, celery, apples, fruit skins, whole berries, olives, many types of candy, marshmallows, raisins, pretzels, and gum. Grapes must be cut vertically before feeding.

Questions and Concerns

My baby will eat only one kind of food. What do I do?

Just like you have your favorite foods, so does your child—except that her favorites change weekly. First, you've got to outsmart her. Here are some suggestions: Take her to the grocery store where she can see a wide variety of colors, shapes, and textures. Disguise foods within others by adding them to soups and stews, and include your child in family mealtimes to expose her to new foods. Entice her with simple foods cut into fun shapes.

What if my baby simply will not eat?

This week your child has gone on a solid food strike after devouring solids for at least a couple of months. First rule out a physical problem such as fever or illness by consulting your doctor. If there is not a medical problem, your baby may just be going through an emotional stage, wanting to be little again and not have to self-feed. Remember, babies will not starve themselves.

Try creative ways of serving your baby food. Involve her in the preparation, use colorful presentations, have her sit with the family, cut food into interesting shapes, or have a picnic indoors or out.

> **Tip:** If your baby is not feeling well, always go back to the first brown rice cereal and serve her a soft and creamy version. It's easy to digest and will help to nourish her.

FOOD INTRODUCTION SUMMARY (WHAT TO FEED AND WHEN)

AGE	9–12 months	9–10 months	11–12 months
FOODS	Yogurt, tofu, pureed legumes (adzuki beans, split mung beans, chickpeas, and lentils), whole grains, pasta, vegetables, fruit, teething toast, tahini, organic poultry.	Yogurt, legumes (pureed lentils, adzuki beans, split mung beans and chickpeas), tofu, noodles (macaroni and shells—non-wheat), poultry.	
GENERAL	Babies can be introduced to a variety of textures. For sore gums, try softer foods. Many teeth are cut at this time, a good time to introduce teething foods. You can also begin finger foods.	When Baby has more teeth you may add a variety of shaped pasta, such as tubes.	More bite-size food and new combinations.

Recipes for Months Nine to Twelve

NEW ON THE MENU

Veggie and fruit combos
Veggie dishes—baked squash and sweet potatoes . . .
Dairy—yogurt with fruit
Snacks—dips and spreads, finger foods
Grains—fruity quinoa . . .
Legumes—tofu, adzuki beans . . .
Meats—organic chicken and turkey with vegetables

TASTY VEGGIE AND FRUIT COMBOS

Sweet vegetables are stars on their own, but mix well with apples or dried apricot to make digestible delights.

Fruit	Vegetable
Apple	Sweet potato Carrot Butternut squash Roasted beet from oven
Dried apricot	Carrot Sweet potato

CHUNKIER PUREES

Sweet potato and apple

- 1 large sweet potato or carrot, washed, peeled, and diced
- 2 apples, washed, peeled, cored, and diced

Boil *enough water in a saucepan to cover the sweet potato and apples.*

Add *sweet potatoes to the boiling water.*

Simmer *for about 8 minutes.*

Add *apples and cook for 10 more minutes.*

Puree, *leaving some chunks.*

Our baby's first apple purees were made from freshly picked orchard apples. Talk about sweet and juicy . . .

Butternut squash and apple

- 1 butternut squash, washed, peeled, and cubed
- 2 yellow delicious, royal gala, or Macintosh apples, washed, peeled, cored, and diced

Boil *a small amount of water in a saucepan.*

Add *squash to the boiling water.*

Simmer *for about 8 minutes or until tender.*

Add *apples and cook for 10 more minutes.*

Puree *using a small amount of cooking water.*

"Bright eyes"

Apricot and carrot

- 1/4 cup dried unsulfured apricots, washed and diced
- 2 medium carrots or 1 large, washed, peeled, and diced

Place apricots and carrot into a saucepan and add just enough water to cover.

Boil, reduce heat to a simmer, and continue to cook for about 15 minutes until soft.

Puree.

Sweet potato and apricot

- 1/4 cup dried unsulfured apricots, washed and diced
- 1 large or 2 medium sweet potatoes, washed, peeled, and diced

Place apricots and sweet potato into a saucepan, adding enough water to cover.

Boil, reduce heat to a simmer, and continue to cook for 15–20 minutes until soft.

Puree, leaving some chunks.

Apple with roasted beets

Booster beets! Beets are high in fiber, iron, and folic acid and are great for the liver, digestion, and immunity.

- 1 royal gala apple or 1 yellow delicious apple, washed, peeled, cored, and diced
- 2 medium beets, washed, with ends cut off

Place beets into a shallow baking dish with a little water.

Roast for about 50 minutes until tender.

Boil apple in a small amount of water for about 10 minutes.

Remove beets from oven and let cool.

Peel and dice beets.

Add beets and apple to a blender and lightly puree.

Naturally sweet!

Beet, apple, and squash

- 1 medium beet, washed, peeled, and diced
- 1apple, washed peeled, cored, and diced
- 1/2 cup of squash, washed, peeled, and diced

Place beets, apples, and squash in a saucepan with enough water to cover.

Boil, reduce heat, and simmer for 15–20 minutes until soft.

Drain vegetables, saving a little cooking water for pureeing if needed.

Puree.

BAKED VEGETABLES

Slowly cooked, oven-roasted vegetables fill your home with delectable aromas and give your baby incredible tastes. These recipes offer a nutritional boost for your kids—high in iron, beta-carotene, and vitamin C.

Baked sweet potatoes

- 2 medium sweet potatoes, washed and poked with a fork

Bake at 375°F for 45 minutes to 1 hour until soft.

Scoop out flesh, mash a little, and serve.

Tip: You may add a little water to the pan and sweet potatoes will stay moist and delicious.

Oven-baked sweet squash
Good enough to lick the plate clean! Hands-down our kids' favorite vegetable.

- 1 delicata (a deliciously sweet small squash) or acorn squash, washed and cut in half. Scoop out seeds.
- Cinnamon (optional after twelve months)

Place squash flesh side down in a ceramic baking dish with a little water.

Cover and bake for at least 40–45 minutes at 375°F until soft.

For younger babies around ten months old, remove flesh and mash; a suribachi works great.

Variation: Mix squash with cooked millet cereal and serve.

YOGURT WITH LIVE AND ACTIVE CULTURES (NINE MONTHS PLUS)
Yogurt makes a great first protein food. It is high in calcium, B vitamins, and supports healthy digestion. It also balances babies' energy and moods. Mixed with sweet fruit it makes a lip-smacking combination.

"Yogurt" does not mean those colorful and cute single packages targeted at kids. They are high in sugar and possibly have artificial colors. The healthiest choice is natural plain bio yogurt (probiotic) without added sweeteners. Full-fat varieties are best for babies; nonfat products are not recommended.

Homemade applesauce with yogurt

- 1/2 cup of yogurt
- 1 tablespoon of homemade applesauce

Mix the yogurt and applesauce together to create a good source of protein and vitamin C treat. You may substitute pear sauce or apple-pear sauce for a delectable treat.

Bananas 'n yogurt

- 1/2 cup of yogurt
- 1/2 mashed banana

Combine yogurt and banana and watch your baby devour.

Yogurt and peaches

- 1/2 cup of yogurt
- 1/2 ripe peach, washed and peeled

Mash the peach with a fork.

Add to the yogurt.

Mango and yogurt

- 1/2 cup of yogurt
- 1 ripe mango washed, peeled, pit removed, and pureed

Mix yogurt and mango together.

Yogurt fruit symphony

- 1 cup of yogurt
- 1/2 cup of pureed fruit (mango, apricot, banana, applesauce)

Mix pureed fruit together and add to yogurt.

Boo-berry yogurt
Babies love the blue color!

- 2 cups plain yogurt
- 1/4 cup blueberries, washed and mashed

Mix these together or add to Baby's cooked cereal.

Fruity yogurt

- 1 banana
- 1/2 cup cooked dried apricots or cooked, dried, and pitted prunes
- 1 tablespoon yogurt

Mash ripe banana and mix with dried fruit puree.

Add to yogurt and serve.

Breakfast blast
An easy meal, high in protein, B vitamins, and vitamin C!

- 1 cup of plain pro-biotic yogurt that contains live and active cultures
- 1/2 cup cooked oatmeal, rice, or millet cereal
- 1/2 cup cooked fruit your choice

Mix together in a blender and enjoy.

TAKE A DIP INTO FUN FOOD!

Yogurt by itself or with fresh fruit puree tantalizes Baby's taste buds. It also goes great with wedges of fruit such as cantaloupe, as well as Baby's favorite vegetables. Steamed bread tastes delicious when dipped in yogurt. Try it with the previous recipes or these new tastes.

Fruity yogurt delights

- Yogurt with banana and peach
- Yogurt with mango and papaya
- Yogurt with fresh berries (strawberries after one year)
- Yogurt with kiwi and apple

SPREADS (TEN MONTHS PLUS) 🌿
Avocado-tahini duet

A creamy delight, high in healthy fats and protein!

- 1/2 teaspoon natural organic tahini
- 1/2 ripe avocado

Mash *1/2 cup of avocado and add 1/2 teaspoon of natural organic tahini and serve.*

Tastes great on a rice cake.

Avocado and tofu

- 1/2 ripe avocado
- 2 ounces of organic soft tofu or organic firm (steam longer)

Steam *tofu for 1 minute.*

Let *it cool for 1 minute and mash with avocado.*

BREAKFASTS FOR THE CHAMPION 🌿
Millet and oatmeal muesli

Packed with natural sweetness, full of B vitamins and iron!

- 3 dried apricots (nonsulfured), chopped
- 1 tablespoon of golden raisins, chopped

- 1 cup of cooked oatmeal cereal
- 1/2 cup of cooked millet cereal

Add *the dried apricots and the raisins to the cooked cereal with a little water.*

Cook *for 15–20 minutes until fruit is soft.*

Fruity quinoa (ten months plus)
Chock-full of protein and vitamin C.

- 1 cup of quinoa rinsed in a strainer until clean
- 1 pear or apple, peeled and diced
- 2 1/2 cups of water

Cook *quinoa and fruit together in a covered saucepan for about 20 minutes.*

Lightly *puree or mash in a suribachi.*

There's plenty for everyone!

Rainbow swirl
A colorful treat for both the eyes and mouth!

- 1 ripe peach, peeled, pitted, and diced
- 1/2 apple, peeled, cored, and diced
- 1/3 cup blueberries
- 1 tablespoon of water

Add *fruit to a small saucepan with water.*

Boil, *reduce heat, and simmer for 5 minutes.*

Mash *with a fork, keep chunky or lightly puree.*

You may add 1 tablespoon of warmed brown rice cereal to thicken for a smooth dessert.

PICK ME UP! FUN FINGER FOODS

- Small cubes of tofu
- Soft cooked pasta noodles, macaroni, or stars
- Ripe fruits, cut into small vertical pieces (grapes, blueberries, cantaloupe, seedless watermelon, ripe peaches, mango, pear, apricot, or plum)
- Natural O's cereal—sugar-free oat (no wheat or corn until one year)
- Soft cooked vegetables in small pieces, such as peas, green string beans, sweet potato, squash
- Soft broccoli or cauliflower—small flowerettes
- Rice cake unsalted and broken into very small pieces
- Cucumber, cut into tiny pieces
- Small fingers of bread that have been lightly steamed
- Zwieback and natural teething cookies

Finger-food safety

Always feed your child in his high chair to prevent him from choking. When he's on the move in his stroller or car seat, you could hit a bump, causing him to choke. Wait until he is finished playing before giving him any finger foods.

Sweet and steamy bread fingers

Scrumptious!

- 1 slice of kamut bread (no wheat until one year)
- 1/4 teaspoon organic tahini (or almond butter after one year)
- 1/8 teaspoon brown rice syrup (optional)
- 1/4 teaspoon homemade apricot or peach puree (optional)

Boil *water in a pot containing a steamer basket.*

Place *bread in a basket and steam on medium heat for about 3 minutes until soft, but not mushy.*

Remove *bread and add your choice of topping, a little tahini and if desired a drop of brown rice syrup or homemade apricot or peach puree.*

Cut *into small fingers and serve.*

Warm 'n toasty nori
Seaweed is high in calcium, iron, and other minerals

• 1 sheet of nori seaweed

Hold *seaweed over a low flame of a gas stove, moving it from side to side. It is done after a couple of minutes when it turns lighter and smells great.*

Rip *into little pieces and put on a plate for your baby.*

Buy pretoasted nori seaweed if you do not have a gas stove.

Small bits of nori mixed into your baby's hot cereal, such as millet, brown rice, or barley, taste delicious.

Millet-squash and nori

• 1 cup squash, butternut or winter, peeled and cubed
• 1/3 cup millet, washed and soaked for at least 3 hours
• 1 teaspoon nori seaweed, toasted, cut into tiny pieces
• 3 cups spring water

Place *millet and squash and water into a medium saucepan and bring to a boil.*

Reduce *heat, cover, and simmer for 30–35 minutes.*

Puree lightly and serve.

Add a few pieces of nori and mix. This mixture becomes firm the next day and may be cut into squares, steamed, and then served as a finger food. Tahini makes a great dip. For toddlers, these squares may be heated in a fry pan on low heat. Delicious!

VEGGIE AND GRAIN DELIGHTS
Creamy broccoli soup
Thick and delicious!

- 2 cups of chopped broccoli flowerets
- 1/2 small onion, diced into small pieces
- 1 cup cooked brown rice cereal
- 3 cups of spring water or vegetable stock

Boil water or vegetable stock.

Add broccoli and onion and reduce heat to a low simmer.

Cook for about 10 minutes.

Add brown rice cereal to pot and remove from heat.

Puree contents on low speed for a minute or two.

Variation for toddlers: add 1/8 teaspoon of mild miso paste. Just stir in at the end of cooking. Spice it up for the rest of the family to enjoy!

Cauliflower and millet
Mashed potato imposter!

- 1 cup millet
- 1 cup cauliflower, cut into small flowerettes
- 4 cups spring water

Wash and drain millet. For extra flavor, dry-roast millet in a pan on low-medium for 3 minutes until it smells toasty.

Add the water and cauliflower and bring to a boil.

Simmer for about 30 minutes until soft and water is absorbed.

Puree.

The consistency of this puree is like mashed potatoes and your baby will love it. It becomes firm the next day and may be cut into little squares and steamed for finger food.

Variation: add 1/2 cup of diced winter squash for sweetness—remember to adjust the water. For toddlers, before serving, mix in a couple drops of sesame oil to add some flavor.

Quinoa with veggies
Protein boost!

- 1/4 cup quinoa
- 1/4 small zucchini, diced
- 1/4 cup butternut squash, peeled and diced
- 1 tablespoon of diced onion
- 1 1/2 cups water

Boil water, add quinoa and onion, and reduce to a simmer for 15 minutes.

Add squash, zucchini and continue to cook on low for 10 minutes until squash is soft.

Puree, leaving a little texture for older babies.

Vegetable stew
Now you've got a way to sneak those veggies into this one-pot delight!

- 1/4 onion, diced

- 1 large or 2 medium carrots, peeled and chopped
- 1 large potato or sweet potato, peeled and diced
- 6 broccoli florets
- 1/2 cup peas, fresh or frozen
- 2 1/2 cups vegetable stock or water

Boil *vegetable stock or water.*

Add *onions, carrots, and potatoes.*

Reduce *heat and let simmer for 15 minutes.*

Add *peas and broccoli and cook for 10 minutes more.*

Mash *or serve chunkier, depending on your child.*

Create new favorites for your baby! Try zucchini, kale . . .

LEGUMES (BEANS, LENTILS, PEAS)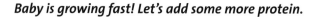

Baby is growing fast! Let's add some more protein.

Once Baby can digest cereals, vegetables, and fruit, proteins come next. Baby's doctor will decide if he is ready at ten months. At this age, babies are typically consuming less milk and the need for new protein sources becomes greater. Legumes are super plant-based sources of protein, high in fiber, and jam-packed with nutrition.

Tofu made from soybeans makes a wonderful first protein. Babies love squishing it between their fingers and relish its spongy texture. Mix it into Baby's grains to boost his protein. Serve tofu a couple of times a week; wait if there is a history of soy allergy. Organic, water-washed tofu is preferred.

For Baby's sensitive tummy, choose adzuki beans, split mung beans, chickpeas, and lentils for easier digestion. Delay other beans such as kidney and navy until after one year, because they tend to be gassy.

Combine legumes with whole grains for complete proteins. These are great protein sources for babies who reject meat. Wait until Baby is three before you feed him peanuts, a legume that is highly allergenic.

Soak legumes in water for at least 4–6 hours, or preferably overnight, to help with digestibility and speed up cooking time. Beans combined with fruit are hard to digest and could cause gas and colic, so that mixture is not recommended.

Try the following recipes at ten months if Baby is ready.

How to cook beans to minimize gassiness

1. Sort the beans with your fingers, removing stones.
2. Soak beans for at least 6 hours or overnight.
3. Discard the soaking water.
4. Add fresh water to the beans.
5. Put a 1-inch piece of kombu in with the beans and boil vigorously for 20 minutes in an open pot.
6. Simmer the beans covered until soft.

Steamed tofu

Baby-approved and #1 play food!

Cut *organic medium or firm tofu into small cubes.*

Place *in a steamer for about 3–5 minutes.*

Cool *and serve as finger food.*

Tofu boosts the protein of any grain and vegetable puree, creating a high-protein treat. Prepare tofu by steaming it or just by adding it raw to these mixtures. Tofu may replace yogurt or cottage cheese in any recipe if your baby's diet is dairy-free.

Tofu 'n peas

• 2 ounces of soft tofu—steamed
• 1 cup of cooked green peas

Mash these ingredients when warm and serve.

Adzuki brown rice

Adzuki beans are small brownish-red beans that are part of the Japanese diet. They are strengthening and nurturing to the kidneys.

• 1 cup brown rice
• 1/4 cup adzuki beans
• 3 cups of water
• 1/2 inch piece of kombu

Soak *adzuki beans overnight or for at least 4 hours and discard soaking water.*

Boil *the beans in the 3 cups of water with kombu.*

Skim *and add the rice after 20 minutes.*

Simmer *until the rice and beans are soft, about 30 minutes.*

Remove *kombu, mash, and serve.*

A pressure cooker may be used to speed up the cooking time, but water needs to be adjusted.

Veggie chickpea rice

• 1/2 cup cooked brown rice
• 1 cup cooked green peas or squash
• 1/2 cup cooked chickpeas

Puree all ingredients once cooked but leave a little texture. A tablespoon of cooking water may be needed.

Golden pea soup
This soup is super sweet and full of protein.

- 1 cup of dried yellow split peas
- 1 medium carrot, washed, peeled, and chopped
- 1 stalk of celery, washed, peeled, and chopped
- 1 teaspoon of chopped onion
- 1 small sweet potato, washed, peeled, and cubed
- 1 fresh sweet corn or 1 cup of frozen corn (only after child is one year and corn has been tolerated)
- 1 small potato washed, peeled, and cubed (after one year)

Boil split peas in water in a large sturdy pot.

Skim the surface and cook for 5 more minutes.

Add vegetables and simmer for 1 1/2 hours.

Puree to a creamy consistency (you may need to drain a little water).

Add some of mother's milk if desired.

For older babies (fifteen months plus), you can sauté the onions in a little bit of good-quality oil for a few minutes before adding the split peas. You may also add a bay leaf and fresh thyme.

Lentil soup (ten months plus)
Packed with iron and protein!

- 1 cup of dried lentils, rinsed
- 1 tablespoon of chopped onion

- 1 stalk of celery chopped
- 1 carrot, cut into thin matchsticks
- 3 1/2 cups of vegetable stock or water
- 1/2 inch piece of kombu

Add *onions to a little boiled water and stir until soft.*

Add *the lentils and vegetable stock or water and kombu.*

Bring *to a boil and cook for about 15 minutes.*

Add *vegetables.*

Simmer *for about 1 hour until lentils are soft.*

Puree *in a blender. (Drain out extra liquid.)*

Lentils and sweet potato or squash

Lentils are rich in iron (important for babies) and fiber.

- 1 cup cooked lentils
- 1 cup cooked sweet potato or squash (save a little water)

Puree *with a little sweet liquid from sweet potato or squash.*

Adzuki bean squash soup

Babies will love this sweet taste!

- 5 cups of water
- 1/2 cup of adzuki beans that have been soaked overnight or for 8 hours
- 1/4 cup of diced onion
- One 2-inch strip of kombu
- 1 cup of butternut or buttercup squash, peeled and cubed

Drain *and discard the water from the beans.*

Boil *the adzuki beans, kombu, and 5 cups of water in a heavy pot.*

Reduce heat, cover, and simmer for about 1 hour.

Add squash and simmer for a further 30 minutes until the squash is soft.

Remove kombu.

Mash a little and serve.

Variation: For toddlers around fifteen months, you may add a pinch of high-quality sea salt.

Theme menu for nine to twelve months: Asian delight
- Millet-squash and nori
- Steamed tofu, or tofu 'n peas
- Toasted nori
- Adzuki brown rice
- Adzuki-squash soup

THE WORLD OF PASTA

Open up a whole new world for mealtimes! Healthy pasta comes in countless varieties. Brown rice, spelt, and kamut pastas taste great, are very nutritious, and can be used instead of wheat (a potential allergen in the first year). Spinach and tomato vegetable pastas, as well as Asian varieties such as soba (buckwheat) or rice vermicelli, make great variations after twelve months.

First noodles (non-wheat, ten months plus)

- 2 cups of noodles made from kamut or brown rice
- 1 cup cooked and pureed vegetables

Boil noodles until soft, drain.

Add cooked vegetables.

MEATS (CHICKEN, FISH, LAMB, BEEF, AND TURKEY)

Just because your baby has teeth doesn't mean that he's ready for meat! Consider your baby's size, digestive maturity, and growth (weight and height). Meats contain complex proteins and are best given after the first birthday, though many babies can be given organic chicken or turkey at ten months. These poultry types are mild tasting, and combine well with sweet vegetables. Fish and red meats can be given after twelve months.

Great fish choices after one year include deepwater whitefish such as Pacific halibut, tilapia, and sole. Herring oil or cod liver oil high in omega-3 (good for Baby's brain) are included after twelve months. Our preference is wild salmon; farmed salmon and rainbow trout may be given occasionally. Keep yourself up-to-date on which fish are the healthiest, as our environment is continually changing. Serve fish poached, steamed, or in a stew. Shellfish is safest after age two or three, whereas sushi or raw fish is best avoided.

Tastes and smells from meats and poultry may cause Baby to reject these foods well beyond the first year. A balanced vegetarian diet can provide a rainbow of nutrients for Baby in the meantime.

Eggs are a common allergen, especially the whites, so it is best to wait until your child is one year old before introducing them. To prepare, scramble the whole egg on low-medium heat until set. Hard-boiled eggs are more difficult to digest. Raw eggs may contain salmonella and should not be given to babies.

My first poultry

Yummy now and after twelve months, just serve these recipes chunkier as your child gets older. Always cook chicken and turkey all the way through, making sure there is no pink, to kill parasites and bacteria.

Chicken or turkey balls

Tender and delicious!

- 2 cups of ground chicken or turkey
- 1 carrot, washed, peeled, and cubed
- 1 stalk of celery, washed, peeled, and chopped
- 1 tablespoon of chopped onion
- 1 potato, washed, peeled, and cubed

Form *meat into small balls and cook with vegetables in a small amount of boiling water about half covered.*

Cover *and simmer for about 1 1/2 hours.*

Break *into small pieces.*

Serve chicken or turkey balls with or without the vegetables. Spice it up a little for Baby's second year.

Variation: *Add cooked brown rice to the uncooked meatballs for texture.*

Poultry puree

- 2 cups of cubed chicken or turkey
- 2 carrots washed, peeled, and diced
- 1 celery stalk washed, peeled, and chopped
- 1 tablespoon of chopped onion

Cook *until soft.*

Puree.

You can substitute lamb for chicken or turkey and spice it up a little after twelve months.

A perfect mix of sweet flavors!

Chicken, sweet potato, and brown rice

Chicken and turkey are rich in protein, B vitamins, and zinc to supercharge your toddler.

- 1/2 cup cooked cubed chicken (The chicken can be boiled or steamed in a small amount of water.)
- 1 cooked sweet potato
- 1/2 cup cooked brown rice cereal
- 1/4 cup applesauce

Puree *all ingredients together in a blender.*

Save a little water from the sweet potato to add for liquid, or use breast milk or formula, if needed.

Turkey sweet rice

All the flavors your baby loves!

- 1/2 cup cooked turkey
- 1/2 cup cooked carrot
- 1/2 cup cooked applesauce
- 3/4 cup cooked brown rice cereal

Puree *to desired consistency.*

Chicken peas 'n rice

- 1 cup cooked frozen green peas
- 1/2 cup cooked chicken, steamed, poached, or roasted
- 1/2 cup cooked brown rice cereal

Puree *to desired consistency.*

Foods for Months Twelve to Eighteen . . . and Beyond

N ow you have a toddler who is a bundle of energy and needs to be fed regularly. Healthy small meals will keep her balanced throughout the day.

Many toddlers will be eating three small meals and two snacks each day. This usually includes at least 3–4 servings of fruits and vegetables and 3–5 servings of carbohydrates per day. Some toddlers will also be eating either 2 servings of vegetable protein (nuts, seeds, legumes, tofu, soy products) or 1 serving of animal protein (fish, chicken, beef, or lamb).

Your child will be introduced to a vast array of new taste sensations during her second year that will establish her future food preferences. If she continues to love whole foods now, these will be the foods she will crave and want to eat as an adult. To reinforce healthy eating habits, follow the same practices as during the nine-to-twelve-months stage. As toddlers model what they see, serve healthy well-balanced meals to everyone in the family.

Part I: Your Twelve- to Eighteen-Month-Old Toddler

DEVELOPMENTAL CHANGES

If your child continued to experience the growth spurts that she had in the first year, she would be a giant by age three! Growth slows down around twelve months, becoming steadier in the second year. As your toddler becomes more active, you will notice that she will begin to lose some of her body fat, and some large muscle development begins.

Many nursed babies reduce or stop breastfeeding on their own around the end of the first year. Some snuggly ones do not want to give up this closeness, and may need lots of extra hugs. Note that "toddler formulas" are no substitute for solid foods, as your child needs to learn how to eat independently.

HOW TO FEED YOUR TODDLER THIS YEAR

Toddlers have tiny tummies and need to be fed every 2–3 hours to energize them. They are always on the go and are busy trying to figure out the world around them. Although some children may have decreased appetites at this time, others, once they begin walking and running, will be ravenous. Other little superheroes are just too active to bother with food. Offer regular mid-morning and mid-afternoon snacks and your toddler will expect this energy and be ready to digest it.

Toddlers' appetites often vary from day to day and one meal to the next, so healthy snacks can help provide the nutrition they need. While occasional snacking is a good idea, make sure your toddler does not become a "grazer" (eating little bits of food all day) because she never eats a full meal. Grazing can interfere with your toddler's daily nutritional requirements, as well as cause other problems. Toddlers should not get into the habit of always having food in their mouths, as this could lead to weight problems later in life. The constant presence of food in the mouth can also lead to tooth decay. Allowing your toddler to "graze" is not ideal; her digestive system will never get a rest nor will her blood sugar stabilize. Give her small regular snacks and meals.

This is also a time to go easy on the liquids. Remember how full you feel after drinking a large bottle of water? Consuming an excess of milk or juice can fill up your toddler, leaving her deficient in many nutrients. Many toddlers may become iron deficient at this time, often because they are drinking too much milk or juice. Typically, a twelve- to twenty-four-month-old toddler should drink no more than about 16 ounces of milk per day. But don't forget to include water.

Toddlers are still looking for oral gratification, especially when teething, so maintain a consistent feeding schedule. Do not give snacks to soothe a crying, bored, or fidgety child unless it is her snack time. Instead, try playing with her or hugging her.

Brendan's a grazer

Ildiko watched her four-year-old nephew Brendan snack all day long during her summer vacation at the cottage. He never sat down for more than a couple of minutes to finish a meal. His mother just fed him small bites of food throughout the day. Ildiko did not want her two toddlers to be "grazers," eating little bits here and there. She enforced small scheduled meals and snacks. Now her preteens are amazing eaters who enjoy healthy regular meals.

Changing taste buds

Some toddlers embrace the new array of foods they can now eat, whereas others refuse anything new, holding on to the tastes and comfort of previous stages. Once they can verbalize *yuk*, mealtimes may never be the same. Toddlers are learning the wonderful skills of self-assertion and mealtime is their classroom.

Many parents remember their babies grabbing the spoon or getting excited as each new taste sensation was introduced. Where did this child go? Be gentle and patient; your baby will see what the family is eating and eventually will want to eat those foods too. Typically, toddlers need to be exposed to a new food about six to twelve times before they will accept it; many parents give up after one attempt. If all else fails, learn how to disguise new foods by adding them to familiar and loved ones. Then try and try again. And remember the story "Green Eggs and Ham" and its last line, "I do so like green eggs and ham!"

New behavior

Your toddler's world has opened up for her as she becomes more active and learns how to walk. Get ready for a whole new set of eating habits during this second year. Toddlers may refuse to swallow or want to hold food in their mouths for what seems like forever. Suddenly, her peas or carrots cannot touch each other or she wants to play rather than eat. Perhaps she will not eat unless served from her favorite bowl or plate.

One trick I had was to have several of the same "favorite" bowl, spoon, and cup on hand. That way, his favorite was always available. (I think this was the only time I was able to outsmart my son.)

Mealtimes and snacks may annoy her because they interrupt her playing and exploring. As toddlers have better memories than babies, they know they will get food all day. She thinks, "I'll just eat later." Some become pickier eaters or less interested in feeding themselves. They may begin to reject or demand certain foods. With a little creativity and patience you can properly nourish your toddler; and most children will eventually outgrow their pickiness. Fear not. Despite her pickiness, your toddler will still grow.

But remember: You're not a short-order cook, ready to change your menu on a moment's notice. If you cater to your toddler now, she will never eat what you serve. This behavior will become even worse when she's three and much pickier.

Introducing allergenic foods

At twelve months, you can slowly begin to introduce those potentially allergenic foods that were withheld during the first year: strawberries, citrus, eggs, cow's milk, goat's milk, soy, tree nuts, seeds, wheat, and chocolate. The exception is peanuts, which should not be introduced until age three. If your child has a strong genetic disposition to a particular allergy, your doctor may also tell you to hold off giving those foods until well beyond the first year, sometimes until age three.

Always wait at least 3–4 days between introducing each new food and always check all of the ingredients first. Don't drop your guard and give your child a piece of food if you don't know all of the ingredients. Commercial baked goods could be contaminated with nuts or peanuts, for example. Although uncommon, it is not unheard of for a child to take one bite of a cookie or pastry in a café and get a full-blown allergic reaction.

Other new foods: poultry, fish, meat, legumes, honey and pure maple syrup, dairy products (cheeses), chocolate

Nightshade vegetables: Tomatoes, white potatoes, peppers, and eggplant may be given slowly and in small amounts. These foods are withheld in the first year because they are hard for babies to digest and frequently cause stomach cramps. (Improper storage of potatoes can increase solanine levels and cause severe gastrointestinal inflammation, diarrhea, or nausea.) On the positive side, when introduced in moderation after the first year, they can be beneficial to your toddler, full of nutrients such as vitamin C and other healthy phytochemicals.

DAIRY PRODUCTS OR NOT?

Dairy products have become a controversial food group. Traditionally, societies in Europe, India, Africa, and North America consumed fresh milk from cows that were hormone, antibiotic, and pesticide free. Though many cultures continue these practices, in North America, this is no longer the case. Raw milk fresh from a farm is difficult to get in North America and in fact is illegal in many states. Milk must undergo pasteurization and homogenization before it is sold to consumers.

Pasteurization is used to destroy any pathogens that the antibiotics have not, and increases shelf life. This process itself is not a problem as it is essentially boiling. However, homogenization, according to many health professionals, changes the composition of the milk, making the fat indigestible. Recently, some health problems have been blamed on milk: cholesterol accumulating in the arteries and heart and lactose intolerance. Some people find that when traveling abroad, they can suddenly drink milk or eat dairy products even though they are usually sensitive to these foods. The lack of these processes may provide an explanation.

Second, milk is usually not consumed in a healthy way, and many people find it difficult to digest. Originally, milk was taken fresh from cows, boiled, sometimes spiced, and served warm, which made it more digestible. Indian cultures add spices such as cinnamon, ginger, nutmeg, and cardamom to warm infant's milk to aid digestion. Today, cold milk is added to cereals or eaten as ice cream; this causes a lot of mucous in the body, especially during winter and spring. Many pediatricians here do not recommend giving dairy products to a child with a cold. Goat's milk is more digestible than cow's milk, and is a better milk option, though it's low in folic acid (which can be obtained in other foods).

If cow's milk is being given to toddlers solely for calcium, there are many alternative foods that provide more absorbable forms of calcium, including dark-green leafy vegetables such as kale, bok choy, seaweeds, whole grains and, when children are older, ground seeds and nuts, canned salmon, and sardines.

Calcium sources

Dairy products contain high levels of calcium that are out of proportion with the other nutrients needed to absorb it, so when people are relying on dairy products as a good calcium source they are not getting a highly absorbable form.

Why is it that in countries such as Japan, which have the lowest dairy-product consumption, osteoporosis levels are low? It may be that calcium is most easily absorbed when nutrients such as magnesium, phosphorus, and vitamin D are present in the right proportions, as commonly found in Japanese diets.

Nondairy sources of absorbable calcium include dark leafy greens, sea vegetables, and almonds.

Some holistic practitioners and pediatricians do not recommend milk or dairy products. There is some research that correlates the onset of childhood asthma and eczema to dairy products. They have found that excess mucous causes recurrent ear infections in some babies that sometimes subside when dairy is removed. Also, keeping an allergic child on milk may deplete their calcium sources. Milk contains very little magnesium and a proper balance between calcium and magnesium assists in calcium absorption. Observe your child closely if you suspect sensitivities to dairy products.

Regardless of your decision about dairy products, it should not form the focal point of a baby's diet. As most mothers will choose to introduce dairy products, some excellent dairy-based recipes are included in this book. As always, keep in mind that the key to nutrition is a varied whole-foods diet including fruits, vegetables, grains, legumes, and moderate amounts of animal products.

Yogurt

You may offer yogurt, a cultured dairy product, at nine to twelve months. Yogurt with bio enzymes is the most easily digested. The beneficial live bacteria (probiotics) have already broken down the milk sugars and digested a lot of the proteins. These special bacteria make it digestible for most babies.

When introducing yogurt, use full-fat varieties because toddlers need healthy fats for brain development. Nonfat products are not recommended for babies. Yogurt and fruit make a tasty combination because it mixes tart with sweet. Use natural plain bio yogurt without added sweeteners.

Cow's milk

If, after the first year, you choose to wean your baby onto cow's milk, organic milk is best. Toddlers do not need to deal with the antibiotics or other chemicals found in conventional milk. Remember to use only whole-fat varieties for children under two years of age, because this fat works with fat-soluble vitamins A and D needed for bones. Skim or low-fat milk, or yogurt, are not for toddlers, regardless of what you consume. However, children can begin to consume 2 percent milk in the third year, provided their pediatrician agrees.

Dairy tips

- Milk is very hard to digest when cold, so bring it to a boil, let it cool and serve.
- Children who cannot digest milk may still be able to tolerate soured milk such as yogurt, kefir, buttermilk, and cottage cheese.
- Goat's milk is healthier than cow's milk, if you choose to give milk.

Colds

During the winter months, if your toddler seems weak and is catching a lot of colds, you may want to supplement her mainly plant-based diet with small amounts of animal products such as chicken soup, eggs, fish, or meat. Your sick toddler may feel stronger from the warmth that these foods provide. Also ensure that you are not feeding her too many fruits, raw foods, or cold drinks at this time, because these can weaken immunity.

CREATING A POSITIVE RELATIONSHIP WITH FOOD

You will quickly learn that if you try to force food on your toddler, you will always lose. Eating should be enjoyable. Have fun with your toddler as you help her become an independent eater. Here are some tips for helping your toddler create a positive relationship with food:

- Teach your toddler how to chew her food slowly and not just swallow.
- Provide your toddler with enough time to eat without rushing her off somewhere.
- Avoid mealtime power struggles. The parent or caregiver thinks, "I am the boss and I make the decisions for when and how much you eat" and the child thinks "I am not hungry."
- Don't take away your child's privileges if she does not eat. "You can't see Grandma until you finish your peas," "no television," "no going to the park," or my favorite, "no dessert."
- Feed your toddler small meals and snacks, remembering that she has a small tummy and is overwhelmed by huge bowls of food.
- Learn to respect your child's appetite. Push her to eat and she may rebel. Toddlers are learning how to self-regulate their own food intake. Scientists are finding that pushing young children to eat more when they say "no" could lead to eating disorders in the future.

- When your toddler seems full, simply remove her plate, but do not replace it with her request for a cookie or a piece of cheese. She will be hungry for the next meal if you don't ruin her appetite.

Try to make food fun for your toddler. Use colorful nonbreakable bowls and containers with compartments to entice your toddler to eat and keep her attention. Television, toys, and games all use bright colors for the same reason.

Your toddler's foods can be more eye-catching and fun than those highly advertised convenience foods (high in fat, salt, and sugar) that you both see on television. You can also sneak vegetables into foods if your toddler begins to reject them. The tasty and colorful recipes in this book will keep your toddler coming back for more.

Jose, age fourteen months, was a poor eater and his caregiver fed him snacks such as cookies in between meals. When he was tired, he would scream for cookies. He would go off and play, but then return and demand more cookies (somewhat like the cookie monster). By the time his father Lopez picked him up from daycare, he was irritable and sleepy.

SUGAR

Toddlers have high energy levels, and whole grains, vegetables, fruit, and good-quality protein help to keep their sugar levels balanced. Toddlers fed an abundance of refined sugars are on an energy seesaw. After a treat they are full of energy, but soon crash. Another treat brings a sugar high and then low. This cycle is unhealthy because a toddler's body, particularly the pancreas, becomes stressed by these sugar surges. Refined sugar also provides empty calories and can rob your toddler of B vitamins. Healthier alternatives, in small amounts, include brown rice syrup or barley malt, pure maple syrup, or pure honey.

Satisfy your toddler's sweet tooth with natural sweet tastes from vegetables such as squash, sweet potato, yams, and fruit. The occasional treat, such as homemade cookies, is fine. Be aware of how food companies market their sugary products to children on television and in grocery stores. Take a proactive approach by teaching your toddler about healthy foods and by picking out healthy foods together.

Sweets are not rewards

Promote healthy eating habits and avoid pacifying your child with treats or junk food when she is upset or hurt. Tell grandparents or relatives to hold the cookies or sweets as rewards when your child performs little songs or begins to walk.

Overeating in adulthood (a learned behavior) may be traced back to food rewards or pacifiers as children. Promising your toddler a treat such as a cookie after she eats her vegetables makes dessert a forbidden and more desirable alternative. Desserts can be a part of a well-rounded meal, but they must not replace the meal.

KITCHEN SAFETY

Most toddlers are very curious about the kitchen and want to help you with food preparation. Go ahead, but just make sure that they do not have access to your knives or other sharp objects, and they are working far away from the stove. Give them simple tasks, such as washing fruit or putting out and arranging cut food into a bowl or fancy plastic container, adding an ingredient, or helping you stir. Let your toddler feel proud and she will be enthusiastic to eat.

Remember to never leave the stove unattended to answer the door or telephone. Keep your knives and appliance cords far away from counter edges, turn pot handles inward, and use back burners on the stove.

Food Introduction Summary (What to Feed and When)

AGE	12 months +
FOODS	Organic poultry, white ocean fish, veal, lamb, all other legumes except peanuts (3 years +), nuts, seeds, eggs, rice milk, almond milk, oat milk , cow's milk, wheat, strawberries, citrus, beef, hard cheese, goat cheese.
GENERAL	Baby may eat mild family foods and some potential allergens.
SPECIFIC MONTHS	**12–18 months** Citrus fruits, strawberries, wheat, cow's milk, eggs, nuts, seeds. Complex proteins, organic poultry, lamb, veal, or white ocean fish. Baby can enjoy foods like casseroles and can chew foods with more texture. He can eat grains of brown rice, quinoa, and millet.

Part II: A Healthy Vegetarian Diet

The benefits of a vegetarian diet begin from an early age. Studies have shown that children fed a plant-based diet have reduced risk of heart disease, lower cholesterol levels (unless genetic), lower obesity rates, and increased health and vitality later in life. Friends and relatives may tell you that your child will not grow properly eating a vegetarian diet because it lacks protein and essential nutrients. You know otherwise. You are not depriving your child when she is eating a diet abounding in natural antioxidants and phytochemicals. Rather, you are giving her the best gift—health. Many children eating conventional diets high in meat and dairy products have been found to be deficient in important nutrients such as essential fatty acids, as well as being anemic and overweight.

Any unbalanced diet, whether plant or animal based, will not properly support your child's growth. A vegetarian diet can be a colorful mosaic of delicious foods, whose variety ensures that your baby receives all the nutrients needed to grow. The American Dietetic Association supports this position. Nuts and seeds in particular contribute valuable nutrients: almonds are rich in calcium, walnuts provide essential omega-3 fatty acids, cashews contain zinc, and Brazil nuts (really seeds) are a great source of selenium (an important antioxidant).

TYPES OF VEGETARIANISM

- **Lacto-ovo** vegetarians eat dairy products and eggs, but avoid all other animal products (meat, poultry, fish, or seafood). It is the most common type and most recommended vegetarian diet by the American Academy of Pediatrics, doctors, and dietitians.
- **Ovo** vegetarians will eat eggs, but no other animal products including dairy products.
- **Vegan** is a strict vegetarian diet that includes no animal products at all, including dairy products, eggs, or bee products (honey). It is the

least recommended diet by doctors and dietitians, as toddlers can become deficient quickly at a time of rapid growth and development. However, many children from seasoned vegans thrive.

- **Modern-day vegetarians** are ones who are vegetarian most of the time, but occasionally eat fish or poultry or both.

RAISING A VEGETARIAN CHILD

Talk to your pediatrician about raising your child as a vegetarian. Many vegetarian mothers go through successful pregnancies and raise healthy vegetarian babies and children. It is very important to monitor a vegetarian child's protein, fat, vitamins and minerals, iron, zinc, vitamin D, and calcium. Plan and organize meals to include essential nutrients and serve a wide variety of plant-based foods, fruits, vegetables, whole grains, legumes, nuts, and seeds. If you plan to eliminate all animal-based food groups, you must be careful to ensure your child's diet contains a wide spectrum of plant-based foods.

Vegetarian children need to be fed calorie-rich foods, including healthy whole fats and proteins for proper growth and development. Serve plenty of essential plant-based fats (critical for brain development) including flaxseeds or flax oil and walnuts. Nuts, seeds, and nut butters are packed with energy and provide essential fats and phytochemicals for your toddler to thrive. Vegetarian children whose diets are high in trans or unhealthy fats, including fast food French fries, and low in essential healthy fats are no better off than their meat-eating friends.

Take your toddler to the farmer's market or grocery store to appreciate the abundance of fresh fruits and vegetables. She will learn that a tasty treat is a bowl of fresh, ripe strawberries or blueberries. A simple and delicious treat can be sweet juicy carrots.

After the first year, children begin to eat foods higher in fiber such as brown rice and other whole grains, raw fruit and vegetables, and lightly steamed vegetables. High-fiber foods are bulky and filling, and should not overwhelm the diet.

When feeding your toddler, consider her genetic makeup and cultural heritage. Some toddlers thrive on a vegetarian diet, but others may benefit from eating a little animal-based food. Some toddlers do better with some high-quality dairy products such as yogurt or goat's milk. Other vegetarian children may need small amounts of white ocean fish and organic poultry or lamb to meet their nutritional needs. Follow your child's lead. If she is lethargic, has no appetite, and shows no other symptoms, it may be a time to check her iron and B_{12} levels, as these are telltale signs. Your pediatrician can determine whether your child needs to take any supplements.

Dietary supplements

Many vegetarian children are given multivitamin and mineral supplements to ensure that they receive all necessary nutrients, especially if they are not good eaters. Some vegetarians supplement their diets with algae such as blue green, spirulina, or chlorella. Each one has a specific function, so before supplementing toddlers, discuss this with your health professional.

For example, some toddlers may get cold when taking blue-green algae, so it may not be appropriate for them. Others who are weak or undernourished may thrive on chlorella supplements. Some vegetarians feed their toddlers nutritional brewer's yeast to supplement their B_{12}. As with any new food, be alert for allergic reactions.

Veggies for Andy

As vegetarians, we wanted to raise our son Andy likewise. Everyone around us seemed to think that he would starve and not grow properly. Our doctor reassured us that a properly balanced vegetarian diet can provide all the necessary nutrients needed for growth. To be on the safe side, he suggested a B_{12} supplement because we would be giving him minimal animal-based products from dairy products and eggs. (Andy is now eighteen and going for his black belt in karate.)

PLANT-BASED PROTEINS

After weaning, vegetarian toddlers rely on a whole-foods diet of legumes, nuts, seeds, whole grains, and green leafy vegetables to satisfy their protein needs. Until recently, most people believed that plant sources of protein were inferior to animal sources. A trip to your local natural foods or grocery store will open your eyes to the abundant plant sources of protein that come from all over the world. For example, quinoa (a grain from South America) is a superb protein source to include in your baby's diet. Take advantage of the vast array of foods used by vegetarians worldwide. Through proper combinations of grains and legumes, excellent-quality plant-based proteins can be provided to the body.

High-quality plant proteins ensure that your toddler will continue to thrive. Not enough protein can lead to sugar cravings and reliance on foods such as fruit juice, which in excess causes your toddler to feel full and eat less. If desired, small amounts of animal products such as dairy products or eggs may be included as sources of complete proteins after the first year.

Beverages such as rice milk are low in protein and must be supplemented with other nutrient-dense proteins.

Soy

In Japan, soy is a very high-quality protein that is usually combined with grains or eaten in soups. However, in North America, soy has become overprocessed and very few reliable sources exist; organic water-washed soy is the best. The soy found in manufactured soy burgers and meat alternatives can be high in salt, fat, and preservatives. Also, many soy milks on the market contain too many sweeteners and highly refined oils. Soy should be given to toddlers in moderation using organic sources. Great soy products include: edamame, good quality miso, and tempeh, which are chock-full of nutrients.

> Kombu is a seaweed that contains natural salts and valuable minerals for your baby. Add tiny amounts to soups, grains, and beans. It is an essential part of a vegetarian diet.

Sprouts: The "Nutritional Superstars"

Sprouts are nutritional powerhouses. They are the result of seeds that have been germinated into living plants. Sprouts may be grown from any seed, including those of nuts, beans, grains, legumes, or grasses such as wheat or barley. They are jam-packed with enzymes, vitamins, minerals, protein, and fiber and contain phytochemicals that have outstanding health benefits. When sprouted these seeds release many nutrients such as sugars, proteins, and fats that become more digestible for your child, and in the case of beans and legumes, less gassy.

Most people's knowledge of sprouts is limited to the common alfalfa sprouts found in the local grocery store, but these are not suitable for babies because they can contain bacterial spores that in excess can be toxic. For a baby, there are a wide variety of suitable sprouts, including sunflower, lentil, pea, and radish to name a few. Sunflower sprouts contain a healthy dose of omega-6 fatty acid.

What is sprouting?

Sprouting occurs when seeds are soaked until they begin to germinate into live sprouts. This process can take from a few days to a week depending upon the seed used. At the end you have a food that has more nutritional value than the seed you started with.

Sunflower, pea, almonds, soybeans, mung beans, millet, lentils, and chickpea seeds are all suitable for sprouting. Flaxseeds are hard to sprout. Seeds must be fresh—rancid seeds will not sprout and shelled seeds will sprout quicker than unshelled seeds.

Chinese physicians have recognized the merits of sprouts for over five thousand years, using them to support health and cure ailments. Sailors in the 1700s suffering from scurvy were treated with sprouts, which are high in vitamin C.

You can buy a good sprouting kit (a Chia Pet or more expensive variety, for example) or use the homemade method described below. Use the same method to sprout all seeds and legumes—all that varies is the time for germination. A sprouting kit is easy to use because you set it up and sprinkle water onto the seeds. Sprouting also makes a great project for your curious toddler.

There are many good references on sprouting, such as Steve Meyerowitz, "The Sproutman." See the back of the book for Website information.

Homemade sprouting method

You'll need a handful of organic unroasted seeds or beans and a large clean glass mason jar that has a screen lid (small holes) and a solid lid. Fill the jar 1/2 full of seeds and add filtered water.

1. Wash the seeds and place in the jar.
2. Fill the jar with filtered water and screw the top on using the screen insert or cheesecloth fastened with a rubber band. (If using cheesecloth, wash before use, making sure it is clean and dry.)
3. Let the seeds soak overnight and drain off the water in the morning.
4. Add fresh water through the screen top to rinse the seeds well.

5. Set the jar on a 45 degree angle to drain as much water as possible and allow seeds to start sprouting.

6. Rinse the seeds about every 4 hours or at a minimum each morning and night.

7. Repeat for 2–6 days until seeds begin to sprout (length of time will depend upon the variety of seed used).

8. Put jar in a window for some direct sunlight.

9. When sprouts are ready to eat (3–5 centimeters long), rinse one last time, replace screen lid with solid lid, and store in the refrigerator. No further rinsing is necessary.

10. Sprouts should be eaten within 2–3 days.

Serving sprouts

Babies must be at least ten months old for sprouts, and they must be served ground. Serve the sprouts blended or pureed with a little water. For nutritious sprout milk, add water to sprouts, puree, and then strain through cheesecloth.

After your child is a year old, most sprouts can be eaten raw, except for the large bean sprouts such as soy, chickpea, split pea, kidney, or other large beans. These may be ground up with water and added to beverages and soups.

VITAMINS AND MINERALS IMPORTANT TO THE VEGETARIAN DIET
Iron

Iron in plant foods may not be as completely absorbed as iron in animal foods. Feed your toddler iron-rich foods, such as beans, whole grains, green leafy vegetables (kale), broccoli, dried fruit (unsulfured apricots and raisins), pumpkin seeds, and blackstrap molasses, many of which contain more iron per calorie than their meat counterparts. It helps to serve foods high in vitamin C together with iron-rich foods to increase iron absorption. Spinach, beet greens, and Swiss chard contain iron, but also a fair amount of oxalic acid, which binds with calcium, interfering with iron absorption. Serve them with high-iron foods.

Vitamin D

Toddlers produce their own vitamin D when their skin is exposed to sunlight. Children eating dairy products also obtain vitamin D from these sources. However, if children are vegan or consume no dairy products, they may need alternate sources from vitamin supplements.

Vitamin B12

Because vitamin B$_{12}$ is found in animal products such as eggs and dairy products, vegan diets will be lacking it. Plant sources including sea vegetables or algae are not reliable sources, but B$_{12}$ can be found in fortified soy products, fortified cereals, and yeast. Vegetarian children may need B$_{12}$ supplements because their bodies have not built up its own stores.

Zinc

This nutrient is usually found in foods that are also high in iron and protein. Zinc can be obtained from legumes, whole grains (not refined), seeds (sesame, pumpkin and sunflower), nuts, and tofu. Therefore, vegetarian diets can contain enough zinc.

Calcium: The way our ancestors got it

Thousands of years ago, our ancestors' diets were rich in calcium foods from plant sources, not animals. Today, cow's milk and other dairy products have been widely advertised and marketed as the best calcium sources. However, many cultures consume no dairy products, but suffer from no deficiencies and very little osteoporosis. True, dairy products are a good source of calcium, but they are not the only or best source.

Proper calcium intake during childhood helps children attain maximum bone mass. Plant foods are superb sources. Look at animals such as elephants, rhinoceros, hippos, and giraffes, which have huge bones, but they get their calcium from plant sources once weaned. After all, we are the only mammals consuming other animals' milk.

Calcium found in plant sources such as dark leafy greens, kale, collards, bok choy, and broccoli is very well absorbed. Nuts such as almonds and seeds (sesame) are very high in calcium. Almond milk makes a wonderful beverage for your toddler. Calcium-enriched soy milk should only be given in small amounts because most are very sweet and contain refined fats (unless you make your own). Calcium-enriched organic tofu is also a good source. Provide your child with a calcium supplement if she does not eat high-calcium plant foods or dairy products.

> *Tip:* Include calcium-rich snacks throughout the day, including shakes, almond butter, or tahini on vegetables.

GOAT'S MILK

Many vegetarian infants and children are fed goat's milk instead of cow's milk. Even though it is deficient in folic acid, it is healthier than cow's milk because it is much easier to digest and higher in fluoride (for growing bones and stronger teeth). Folic acid can be obtained from other foods such as dark-green leafy vegetables and egg yolks. However, in North America most people drink pasteurized goat's milk, which destroys a lot of the fluoride.

CHOCOLATE

Chocolate has always been a desired food since the time cacao beans were used as currency by the Aztecs in Mexico. Today in North America people eat so much chocolate it could almost be considered one of the food groups! People all over the world, from Europe to Asia, love it. Recently, scientists have found that cocoa contains beneficial antioxidants. It also contains beneficial nutrients such as calcium, magnesium, and vitamins A, B, C, and D.

Provide your toddler with small quantities of the best quality: real chocolate that is organically grown with a high percentage of cacao, around 70 percent. Teach your child to savor a piece and not devour a whole bar.

If your child has a nut allergy or is potentially allergic to nuts, read chocolate labels carefully. Some kids have adverse reactions to the chocolate itself, but most often it is not a reaction to the pure stuff. They usually have consumed overly processed chocolate that is high in fat, trans fats, and full of refined sugar, but very low in the good stuff, cacao. Keep in mind that it is an allergenic food, so monitor your child's first taste. Even good-quality chocolate contains some sugar, so limit the amount your kids eat, and do not serve close to bedtime because it contains caffeine.

"Cooking is at once child's play and adult joy. And, cooking done with care is an act of love."

—Craig Clairborne

chapter 14

Recipes for Months Twelve to Eighteen . . . and Beyond

WHAT'S NEW ON THE MENU?

Seasonings: mild flavors
Beverages: almond milk, amasake, kukicha tea, smoothies, fruit blenders
Appetizers: dips, hummus
Grains: basmati rice
Breakfasts: French toast, muesli, rice pudding
Deserts: cinnamon baked apples, baked custard, apple-pear crumble
Lunch: egg pizza, trees 'n cheese, mashed potatoes
Dinner: noodles 'n sauce, baked salmon, butternut squash soup,
*   shepherd's pie*

Now that your baby has become a toddler, the range of foods that he can enjoy has greatly expanded. The delicious recipes in this section will tantalize your child's taste buds, but feel free to improvise and add your own personal loving touch.

If your toddler has become a little tired of the milder tastes from Mom's menu and you have run out of creative ways to serve certain foods, don't fret. These new recipes will spice things up! When children are exposed to a wide variety of tastes when they are young, they tend to be less fussy about food later.

FLAVORFUL ADDITIONS
Sautéed onions

As they cook, onions become super sweet, adding new depth and flavor to your toddler's meals. Sauté onions in a tiny amount of organic cold-pressed oil cooked on medium heat. Combine these onions with carrots and celery for a delicious base for soups.

> It's best to sauté vegetables with oil on medium heat because high temperatures can cause harmful chemicals to be formed in the food.

Ghee

Clarified butter, or ghee, adds creamy buttery flavor to grains, warm milk, steamed vegetables, soups, and stews. Nourish your children and help strengthen their vitality with ghee. To make ghee, melt butter gently in a small heavy saucepan. The butterfat will separate and the milk solids will sink to the bottom of the pan. When white foam forms on the top, simply remove the pot from the heat and skim the foam off. What you are left with is delicious and nutritious ghee.

SEASON IT UP!

We are not talking about bringing on the hot sauce quite yet. Try adding a little salt with miso paste, tamari (natural soy sauce without preservatives), high-quality sea salt (SI or Celtic), or gomashio (crushed sesame seeds). Sea vegetables naturally salt baby's food, providing calcium, iron, and trace minerals. When Baby's ready for a little spice in his life, cinnamon or herbs such as basil and thyme may be used in tiny amounts.

Gomashio

Gomashio ("Goma" means sesame and "shio" means salt) is a common Japanese condiment made from crushed sesame seeds and sea salt. It's easy to prepare and versatile. Sprinkle it on your toddler's rice, oatmeal, vegetables, and soups. Make a fresh batch every few days and store in a sealed glass jar. Enjoy it yourself!

- 1/3 teaspoon of sea salt
- 10 teaspoons of sesame seeds

__Roast__ the sea salt in a cast-iron skillet over medium-low heat, stirring it continually for about 2 minutes.

__Place__ roasted salt in a suribachi.

__Rinse__ sesame seeds with water in a fine mesh strainer.

__Dry roast__ them in the same skillet, stirring them constantly until they are light brown and most have popped.

__Add__ roasted sesame seeds to the suribachi and finely grind (about 3–4 minutes).

BRAIN GRAINS

Because grains contain complex carbohydrates, they are energizing and also calming at the end of the day. Refer back to the first recipes for grains; you will be soaking brown rice and barley for less time and cooking in less water. The consistency of the grains will be thicker for your toddler and some will be able to handle soft whole grains.

Basmati rice—a taste of India

Fragrant and delicious! Baby's first grain in India; it's easy on the tummy and full of nutrition.

- 1 cup of basmati rice (for brown rice, soak for an hour and increase the water by 1 cup)
- 2 1/2 cups of water
- 1/4 tsp of ghee (optional)
- pinch of sea salt

Wash *rice well.*

Boil *rice.*

Add *salt and ghee (if desired).*

Simmer *for 30 minutes or until water is absorbed (longer for brown rice—45–50 minutes).*

MUNCHIES (TODDLER SNACKS)

Feed your toddler every two to three hours, because he is on the move and growing fast. Healthy and nutritious whole foods and complex carbohydrates are what he needs. He won't miss junk foods because they give him sugar bursts and then energy lows, which makes him cranky.

- Vegetable sticks—celery, grated carrot, peppers, cucumber
- Fruit slices—soft pieces of ripe pear, banana, mango, cantaloupe
- Dips such as yogurt or tahini for fruit and vegetables
- Box of raisins
- Rice cakes

- Rice balls (see recipe) eighteen months plus or earlier if broken into smaller pieces
- Cubes of steamed tofu
- Oat cereal—natural no-sugar "Oatios"
- Small clumps of grains such as brown rice
- Soft, cooked whole-grain pasta noodles, macaroni
- Zwieback
- Toasted whole-grain bread cut in squares topped with almond butter or melted cheese
- Steamed vegetables—broccoli, cauliflower, carrot, green beans, or peas
- Lightly mashed hardboiled egg or scrambled egg

Unleash your imagination! Create meals that will keep your baby at the table and eating. Vegetables, fruit, and cheese can be organized onto platters and into designs that will keep your baby's attention. Our family regularly invited broccoli man, robot man, pumpkin lady, and monster man for dinner. And as your kids get older, they can create their own designs.

NEW BEVERAGES

Amasake (sweet rice beverage) is a wonderful treat; serve it diluted. It is commonly found in natural food stores.

Kukicha tea (Japanese twig tea) is a healthy warm drink; make it weak. This tea is available in Asian or natural food stores.

NUT AND SEED MILKS

Build me up! Nut and seed milks are super-high in bone-building calcium and protein.

Almond milk

Yummy in smoothies and in hot cereals. Almond milk is naturally sweet.

• 2 cups spring water or purified water
• 3–4 tbsp raw almonds, roast them a little yourself

Soak *almonds in the water for at least 6 hours, preferably overnight.*

Peel *the almonds by rubbing them between your fingers (or add almonds to boiling water and let cool).*

Add *the almonds and the soaking water to the blender and grind, starting at low speed and increasing to high until smooth.*

Pour *through a fine mesh strainer to catch any pieces.*

For extra sweetness, you can add 1–2 teaspoons of brown rice syrup or pure maple syrup.

Almonds are rich in bone-building minerals, calcium, magnesium, brain-boosting B vitamins, and omega-6 fatty acids.

Seed milk

• 1/4 cup pumpkin, sesame, or sunflower seed
• 1 cup of room temperature spring water

Soak *seeds in water overnight.*

Drain *seeds and throw away soaking water.*

Add *new water to the seeds, and blend.*

Strain *for babies at one year (toddlers at two years may get used to unstrained).*

Pumpkin seeds are a superfood containing both omega-3 and omega-6 fatty acids.

Almond butter (fourteen months plus)

A calcium and protein boost and high in brain builders omega-3 and omega-6.

- 1 1/2 cups of raw almonds (fresh)
- 1/2 teaspoon of flaxseed oil
- 1/2 teaspoon of sunflower oil
- pinch of good-quality sea salt (optional)

Toast almonds lightly in a dry fry pan over medium-low heat for 3–4 minutes, stirring constantly until golden brown.

Pour into a bowl to cool.

Place the toasted almonds, oils, and sea salt (if using) into a food processor and blend until creamy.

Store in a glass jar in the refrigerator.

Scrumptious on toast or rice cakes and in cereals! Homemade never tasted so good.

Brown rice balls (eighteen months plus or earlier if broken into smaller pieces)

High in B vitamins, calcium, protein, and minerals. You'll love them too!

- 1 cup of cooked brown rice, soft and at room temperature or warm
- 11/2 teaspoons of gomashio (toasted crushed sesame seeds)
- 1/4 sheet of toasted nori seaweed in thin strips

Moisten your hands and take a little cooked rice.

Form the rice into golf ball–sized balls.

Wash your hands.

Roll *each rice ball in crushed sesame seeds.*

Wrap *a thin strip of nori around each rice ball.*

Variations: *Substitute ground or crushed toasted pumpkin seeds or almonds; or push a little almond butter into the middle of the rice ball after you roll it; or use a brown rice and millet combo (or just millet).*

SMOOTHIES AND FRUIT BLENDERS

Watch your little one smile as he sips these frothy delights through a straw. Smoothies and fruit blenders are a meal in a glass—high in protein, fiber, and vitamins. So you say your child won't eat anything and you're worried about his nutrition—watch him devour these!

Smoothies are thick shakes that usually contain some form of milk; fruit blenders have juice as their base. Serve them as snacks and pump up that fruit and fiber! Cool them down in the summer by adding some frozen bananas. Toddlers love to invent new combos using their favorite foods; try pineapple, melons, fresh apricots, or peaches.

Strawberry-nana smoothie

- 1/4 cup fresh strawberries
- 1 banana
- 1 cup milk (goat, cow, soy, or rice)

Place *all ingredients into a blender.*

Blend *until smooth and creamy. During the heat of summer you may throw in a couple of ice cubes or use a frozen banana to cool those little ones.*

Strawberries are rich in vitamin C, a wonderful antioxidant that also boosts children's immunity.

Strawberry and banapple splash

• 1/4 cup of fresh strawberries
• 1 medium banana
• 1 cup of apple or pear juice

Blend *all ingredients together on medium heat until smooth.*

For toddler's digestion

Yogurt with live active cultures provides the intestines with healthy bacteria needed to help digest food properly. If your child has been treated with antibiotics, it can aid in restoring the intestinal flora in the intestines.

Blueberry moo

• 1/3 cup blueberries
• 1 banana
• 1/2 cup plain yogurt
• 1/2 cup milk or apple juice

Blend *all ingredients together till smooth.*

Blueberries are rich in vitamin C, an excellent antioxidant that helps protect the brain from free radicals and toxins.

Orange and banana cream

• 1 seedless orange
• 1 medium banana

- 1/2 cup of plain yogurt
- 1/2 cup of orange juice

Blend all ingredients together in a blender until creamy.

Mmmango blast

Mangos are rich in vitamin A (essential for healthy eyesight and skin), as well as powerful antioxidant vitamins C and E, beta-carotene, and fiber.

- 1 mango, diced
- 1 banana
- 2 tablespoons of yogurt
- 1/4 cup of peach or mango juice
- 2 ice cubes

Blend all ingredients until smooth and serve.

Pineapple Lassi

Also known as just a lassi in countries such as India, Sri Lanka, Indonesia, and Malaysia. Great summer coolers!

- 1/2 cup of fresh pineapple, diced
- 1/2 mango, diced
- 1/2 banana, diced
- 1 tablespoon of yogurt
- 1/4 cup of orange juice, fresh squeezed
- 2 ice cubes

Blend all ingredients until smooth.

Purple peach

- 1 peach, peeled and diced
- 2 tablespoons of yogurt

- 1/2 cup of fresh blueberries
- 1/4 cup of pear or peach juice

Blend *until creamy.*

Triple-berry breeze

- 1/3 cup of blueberries
- 1/2 cup of strawberries
- 1/3 cup of raspberries
- 1/2 cup of peach or apple juice

Blend *all ingredients until smooth and serve.*

Banana soy twister

- 1 banana
- 1 date
- 1 cup of soy milk
- pinch of cinnamon (optional)

Blend *all ingredients together and serve.*

Apple berry booster

- 5 strawberries
- 1 apple, peeled, seeded, and cubed
- 2 tbsp soft tofu
- 1/2 cup of apple or pear juice

Blend *all ingredients together and serve.*

Tropical treat

- 1 seedless orange

- 1 medium banana
- 1 mango
- 2 cups fresh orange or apple juice

Blend all ingredients until smooth. Enough to share!

JUICE IT UP!

Fresh juices are quick and nourishing energizers for your growing toddler, packed with vitamins, minerals, and enzymes. Your toddler can have small servings (4–5 ounces or about 1/2 cup) of juice, limited to 2 serving per day. Be creative! Try different combinations and sneak in some greens, like adding a sprig of parsley to carrot juice. Always serve juices immediately after preparation to reap their full benefits.

Tips: Use organic fruits and vegetables if possible (if not organic, peel off the skin). Remove any bruised areas, core fruit, and peel citrus.

Carrot

- 1 large organic carrot

Juice and dilute with a little water and serve!

Carrot and apple

- 1 medium-large organic carrot
- 1/2 apple, cut into wedges

Juice and serve immediately.

Apple

- 1 sweet apple (golden delicious, royal gala), cut into wedges

Juice and serve.

Apple and pear

- 1 ripe pear, cut into wedges
- 1 apple, cut into pieces

Juice and serve immediately.

Orange juice

- 2 oranges

Peel oranges.

Put oranges through the juicer, dilute with a little water, and serve.

TAKE A DIP (FOURTEEN MONTHS PLUS)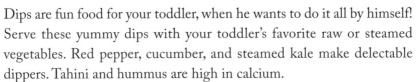

Dips are fun food for your toddler, when he wants to do it all by himself!
Serve these yummy dips with your toddler's favorite raw or steamed
vegetables. Red pepper, cucumber, and steamed kale make delectable
dippers. Tahini and hummus are high in calcium.

Creamy tahini dip

1/4 cup of spring water mixed with 1 teaspoon of freshly squeezed lemon
juice, 1 teaspoon tahini (sesame butter), 1/2 teaspoon brown rice syrup, or
barley malt (optional).

> Tahini, which is a ground sesame seed paste, seems to be loved
> by babies. It goes well with vegetables such as broccoli. Our son
> loved a combination of broccoli, tofu, and tahini. It also mixes
> well with chickpeas to make hummus.

Natural yogurt

Serve plain or with homemade fruit puree.

Hummus (sixteen months plus)

- 1 cup of raw chickpeas, or organic canned chickpeas (cooked; no preservatives)
- 1 teaspoon–1 tablespoon of organic tahini
- 2 tbsp lemon juice
- 1/2 clove of garlic (optional)
- 1 tablespoon of olive oil
- pinch of salt
- water to thin

Soak *raw chickpeas overnight or for at least a few hours.*

Add *a piece of kombu.*

Boil *until very soft with a small piece of kombu (when soft, they mash easily).*

Drain *chickpeas (or start with cooked chickpeas at this point).*

Remove *kombu.*

Puree *chickpeas, tahini, lemon juice, olive oil, garlic, and salt.*

Serve with cooked or raw vegetables, as a dip or on steamed bread or rice cake.

Theme menu for twelve to eighteen months: Middle Eastern

- Hummus with vegetables, cucumber, red pepper to dip
- Sweet roasties (see this chapter for recipe)

- Lentil soup
- Sautéed bananas
- Fruit chunks

My first salsa (sixteen months)

- 1 medium tomato, chopped
- pinch of sea salt
- 1/4 teaspoon of fresh cilantro, chopped
- 1 teaspoon of lime juice

Blend *in a food processor and serve with rice cakes.*

FRUITY DESSERTS

Satisfy that sweet tooth—dessert doesn't have to mean sugary treats! Feel good about dessert again and enjoy one yourself.

Cinnamon baked apples

Pop them in the oven 25 minutes before you sit down to feed your toddler and family. The wonderful aroma will fill your home, and your toddler won't be able to resist. "An apple a day" never tasted so good!

- 3 large apples with tops cut off and cored, leaving the bottom intact
- 1 tablespoon or a handful of raisins
- pinch of cinnamon for each apple
- 3 tablespoons of water
- 1 tablespoon of brown rice syrup or pure maple syrup (optional)

Fill *apples with raisins, cinnamon, and sweetener if you desire.*

Place *the tops of the apples back on.*

Bake at 375°F for about 40 minutes until soft. After cooking for 20 minutes, you may cover the apples so they become juicier.

Or try this: After baking, let apples cool for a few minutes, peel away skin and mash them to create scrumptious "Baked applesauce."

Peachberry

- 1 large peach, peeled, pitted, and diced
- 1/3 cup fresh strawberries, hulled and halved

Place the fruit into a small saucepan.

Add a little water and bring to a boil.

Reduce heat to a simmer and cook for 4 minutes.

Drain off excess liquid and mash.

Puree with a teaspoon of brown rice cereal if your toddler likes smoother purees.

Over the rainbow

A fruity dessert that will have them asking for more. Use seasonal fresh fruits and try your own combinations.

- 5 cherries, halved and pitted
- 1/3 cup of blueberries
- 1 peach or 2 apricots, peeled and diced
- 1 tablespoon of water

Boil water and fruit in a small saucepan.

Reduce heat and continue to cook for 4–5 minutes.

Puree, leaving some chunks.

Sauteed bananas (eighteen months)

Delicious on its own or as a topper!

- 2 small or 1 large banana, cut into small pieces
- 1/2 teaspoon of cinnamon
- 1/2 teaspoon of good-quality olive or vegetable oil

Heat *oil on medium-low and sauté banana for 2 minutes.*

Sprinkle *with cinnamon.*

Serve *over French toast or on top of cereal.*

Bananas are rich in potassium, soothing to the tummy and calming.

Apple-pear crumble

Your toddler's first (and soon-to-be favorite) crumble. So good and nutritious that you won't feel guilty about serving it for breakfast.

- 1 apple, washed, peeled, cored, and diced
- 1/2 pear washed, peeled, cored, and diced
- 2 teaspoons of raisins
- 1 tablespoon of ground oats (from blender)
- 1/8 teaspoon cinnamon
- 1 teaspoon of cold butter

Preheat *oven to 375°F.*

Place *apple and pear into a saucepan.*

Add *water to cover halfway.*

Add *the raisins and cinnamon and bring to a boil.*

Reduce *heat and simmer for 5 minutes.*

Pour the mixture into two ramekin (custard cup) containers.

Add the butter to the oats and blend by hand.

Sprinkle this oat topping onto the apple-pear mixture and bake for 20–25 minutes.

More wonderful crumble combos to wow them: pureed apricots or peaches-apple, strawberry-apple, apricot-apple, blackcurrant-apricot.

Golden apple pudding

More pudding please!

- 3 apples washed peeled, cored, and diced
- 1/2 cup of apple juice
- 1/2 cup of rolled oats
- 3/4 cup of cooked brown rice
- 1/2 teaspoon of brown rice syrup or pure maple syrup
- pinch of cinnamon
- 1/2 cup of water

Place all ingredients into a heavy saucepan with water and bring to a boil.

Reduce heat and simmer for 25–30 minutes.

Puree in a blender.

Seasonal apricot or peach puree brings new taste sensations to this dessert.

CUSTARDS
Baked custard

Think of this as crème brulee without the sugar topping. Baked custard once appeared on nursery menus everywhere, but has been lost in recent years. It's creamy, sweet, and loaded with protein. Take it out of hiding and your toddler will love you. Don't forget to make extra for you to enjoy when he's asleep. Add a pure sugar topping if you like (but be careful with that blow torch or just put it under the broiler). You deserve a treat!

- 2 large eggs
- 2 cups of milk, rice, soy, or goat's
- 1/4 cup maple syrup or 1/2 brown rice malt
- 1 tsp vanilla

Preheat *oven to 325°F.*

Blend *all ingredients with a whisk or hand mixer.*

Place *mixture into custard cups (ramekins) or a shallow baking dish*

Set *ramekins into a water bath in a large pan to cover 1/2 to 3/4 way.*

Bake *for 1 hour. Insert a knife or toothpick and if it comes out clean, it is ready.*

Veggie custard

An ingenious and delicious way to hide those veggies!

- 2 egg yolks
- 1 large egg
- 1 cup of organic milk
- 3/4 cup of cooked pureed vegetables, broccoli, carrot, green beans
- 1/2 teaspoon olive oil

Preheat *oven to 350°F.*

Oil *2 custard cups or ramekins.*

Beat *the egg and egg yolks and add the milk and pureed vegetables.*

Split *into the 2 custard cups.*

Set cups in hot water in a large pan to cover 1/2 to 3/4 way.

Bake in the oven uncovered for about 25 minutes until set. Insert a knife or toothpick and if it comes out clean, it is ready.

Cool for 5 minutes.

You may substitute different vegetables such as zucchini or green peas.

PUMP ME UP! BREAKFAST IDEAS YOUR BABY WILL DEVOUR

You know that they'll be running circles around you all day. Do they really need more energy? Of course they do! Delicious ideas: French toast, porridge, yogurt with pureed fruit, muesli, "how the egg got into the toast," scrambled egg and rice pudding, yogurt with pureed fruit.

Toddler muesli (eighteen months plus)

No-mess, no-fuss protein booster.

- 1 cup of long cook oatmeal flakes soaked overnight with a splash of natural orange or apple juice
- 1/4 cup dried raisins, diced
- 4 dried apricots, diced
- 1 tbsp ground almonds or sunflower seeds
- 1/3 cup apple washed, peeled, cored, and diced

In the morning mix with 1/4 cup yogurt and serve.

Or, you can cook soaked oat mixture with water, boil, then simmer for about 20 minutes. When cooled, mix with yogurt and serve.

Peach sunrise (sixteen months plus)

• 1 cup of long-cook oatmeal flakes
• 1/2 fresh peach or 1 apricot, peeled and diced (near end of cooking)
• or 3 dried apricots, chopped, or a few raisins (beginning of cooking)
• 2 cups of water

Bring *water and oatmeal to a boil.*

Simmer *until soft.*

Add dried unsulfured apricots or a few raisins at the beginning of cooking or fresh cut-up peaches or apricots toward the end of cooking.

Sprinkle with freshly ground flaxseed to add omega-3 for healthy brain and eyes.

> Oats are the perfect breakfast food, as they combine B vitamins, carbohydrates, fiber, iron, and zinc to keep your toddler balanced and energized all morning.

Fruit 'n yogurt

• 1/2 cup of yogurt with live, active cultures
• 1 tablespoon of toddler's favorite fruit puree (apricot, etc.), or simply mash some banana.

Combine *ingredients and serve.*

Brown rice pudding

Please your toddler with the ultimate comfort food. For older toddlers, add some chopped, pitted dates; experiment with favorite fruits; and add a little cinnamon. Slow-cooking brings back that old-fashioned taste we love.

- 2 cups of brown rice, cooked
- 1 cup of milk—rice, oat, soy
- 1 tablespoon of brown rice malt or brown rice syrup
- 1 egg

Combine *all ingredients.*

Bake *at 350°F for 30 minutes until lightly browned.*

Basmati rice pudding (sixteen months plus)
Bring the wonderful aromas and flavors of the East into your kitchen.

- 1 cup of basmati rice (may be presoaked for 1 hour for easier digestion)
- 1 tablespoon of golden or black Thompson raisins
- 1–2 teaspoons of ground almonds
- 1/2 tablespoon of chopped dried apricots
- 1/4 teaspoon pure vanilla (optional)
- 1/4 teaspoon cinnamon
- 1/4 teaspoon of brown rice syrup or pure maple syrup
- 3 cups of water
- 1 cup of whole milk

Rinse *rice in cold water until water becomes clear.*

Boil *water in a heavy medium-sized saucepan and add rice.*

Simmer *for 15 minutes.*

Add *the remaining ingredients.*

Simmer *for another 15 minutes until rice is soft and all liquid is absorbed.*

Remove *from heat and keep covered, allow rice to steam for a few minutes.*

Stir and serve.

Top with fruit puree if desired.

Try this delicious topping: 1/2 teaspoon of homemade or all-natural (no sugar) chunky fruit puree: blueberry, apricot, strawberry. (See chunky puree recipes.)

French toast (sixteen months plus)
Satisfy even the pickiest eater with this recipe! Some toddlers like to call it "eggy bread."

- 1 slice of whole-grain bread
- 1 egg
- 1 tablespoon of milk (optional)
- pinch of cinnamon for a topping

Heat a fry pan on medium heat with a few drops of vegetable oil.

Beat egg with milk (optional).

Add bread, soak for 20 seconds on each side, and place in fry pan.

Cook on both sides until the egg is set.

Cut into long fingers, sprinkle with cinnamon and serve.

Serve with a dip such as fruit puree and yogurt; or top with a tiny bit of pure maple syrup or sautéed bananas.

How the egg got into the toast (sixteen months plus)
Named by my kids, this recipe is still a household favorite. They thought it was magic every time. High in protein and B vitamins to pump them up for the day.

- 1 egg

- 1 piece of whole-grain toast
- 1/4 teaspoon of olive oil

Cut *a small circle out of the middle of the bread, big enough for an egg to fit inside (use the rim of a cup or a cookie cutter).*

Heat *a fry pan on medium heat and add olive oil.*

Place *the bread in the pan and crack the egg into the hole.*

Cook *on one side, flip carefully, and cook on the other side until the egg is cooked, not runny inside.*

LUNCH RECIPES: QUICK AND EASY SUGGESTIONS FOR WHEN YOU'RE ON THE GO

Egg pizza (sixteen months plus)

Baby's first pizza.

- 2 eggs, beaten well
- 1 tbsp of grated cheddar or mozzarella cheese (optional)

Pour *a little good-quality oil (olive) into a heated fry pan.*

Add *beaten eggs to pan and make an omelet.*

Cut *it into pizza slices.*

If using cheese, top omelet just before eggs set.

Cheesy scrambled eggs

- 2 eggs, beaten well
- 1–2 tbsp grated cheese

Put *a little good quality oil (olive) into a heated fry pan.*

Lightly scramble eggs on medium heat; when eggs are almost done, add the cheese and serve.

Make sure that the eggs are fully cooked and not raw inside.

> Eggs are nutritional wonders in a small white package: high in B vitamins, iron, and protein; memory enhancers; and also great energizers. They are high in vitamin K (for growing bones) and selenium (an antioxidant). Choose organic free-range eggs, high in omega-3.

Creamy soba with tahini

Yummy! Our son loved this mixed with small pieces of avocado.

- 1 cup of soba (buckwheat) noodles
- 3 cups of water
- pinch of sea salt
- 1 tablespoon of tahini

Boil water and salt.

Add soba noodles.

Cook for a few minutes until soft.

Drain noodles.

Mix with tahini and serve.

BEAN DISHES

Beans are high in protein, fiber, and complex carbs; they provide long-lasting energy for your active toddler. Beans also bring to mind the old saying that it all boils down to gas (the last thing we want our baby to get). Use only the suggested beans (adzuki, lentils, split mung, and chickpeas), follow these recipes, and you're in the clear.

Adzuki-squash

Sweet and scrumptious! Great for the whole family

Adzuki beans are part of the Japanese diet and are small brownish-red beans that strengthen and nurture the kidneys. Sweet squash is wonderful for the spleen, stomach, and pancreas and is a natural sweetener that does not cause spikes in blood sugar. Together, they are a perfect match.

- 1/2 cup of adzuki beans, soaked for 6–8 hours or overnight
- 4 inch piece of kombu, soaked, and cut into 1-inch squares
- 1 cup of buttercup squash or other hard winter squash, peeled, and cut up into chunks
- pinch of high-quality sea salt
- water

Discard soaking water from beans.

Put kombu into a heavy saucepan and place squash on top.

Add adzuki beans on top of the squash.

Pour in enough water to just cover the squash, but not the beans on top.

Bring to a boil uncovered, then cover and simmer on medium-low heat for at least 1 1/2 to 2 hours until beans are soft.

Add a pinch of sea salt and simmer for another 30 minutes until the beans are mushy and most of the liquid is absorbed. A little more water may be needed if it gets too low; check every 8–10 minutes.

Mash a little more if needed and serve.

Red magic stew

Amaze your toddler by how the lentils are red to start, but turn yellow and mushy when cooked. Spice some up in another pot and give yourself a boost.

- 1/4 cup red lentils
- 1/4 chopped onion
- 1/3 cup of red pepper, chopped
- 1 1/2 cups vegetable, chicken stock or water
- 1 medium carrot
- 1 diced plum tomato (optional)
- 1 teaspoon of olive oil
- 1/3 teaspoon of herbamare seasoning

Sauté *onion with oil in a saucepan on medium heat.*

Add *the carrot, red lentils, red pepper, seasoning, and stock or water.*

Boil *and reduce heat; cover and simmer for 30 minutes.*

Mash *or puree lightly to blend ingredients.*

Lentils are rich in iron, protein, B vitamins, and fiber. A great energy source for growing toddlers.

Baby dahl (fourteen months plus)

- 1/2 teaspoon vegetable oil
- 1/4 small onion, diced
- 1/2 cup of carrot, diced
- 1/2 cup of sweet potato or potato, peeled and diced
- tiny pinch of cumin or coriander (optional)
- 1/2 cup of dried red lentils (4 ounces), rinsed
- 3 cups of water or vegetable stock

Heat the oil in a pot on medium heat and sauté onion for 2 minutes until soft.

Add the carrot and sweet potato or potato.

Add the water or vegetable stock and red lentils and bring to a boil.

Simmer for 30 minutes until the lentils are soft.

Let it cool for 5 minutes.

Drain any excess water.

Mash in the pot or take a small amount out and mash in the suribachi (best way), or puree in a blender or use a hand blender, leaving some chunks, or puree longer for those toddlers who still like soft purees. Keep it chunkier for babies closer to eighteen months and you may also a little more spice—turmeric, cumin, and coriander are commonly used in this recipe.

Serve with rice for a complete protein!

Toddler kichadi (an East Indian delight)

A complete protein dish that is easily digestible.

- 1 cup basmati rice
- 1/2 cup split mung beans (found in natural food markets or Asian food markets)
- 1 tsp ghee
- pinch of cumin
- pinch of turmeric
- 4 cups of water

Rinse rice and mung beans well.

Place all ingredients in a medium saucepan.

Bring *to a boil and reduce heat.*

Simmer *for 25–30 minutes or until beans are soft and rice is cooked.*

Serve. *You may mash a little with a fork or in a suribachi.*

> Theme menu for twelve to eighteen months: South Asian
> - Basmati rice
> - Baby dahl
> - Sweet potato fries with mild spices
> - Mango lassi

VEGGIES ON THE SIDE
Trees 'n cheese

Just a spoonful of cheese helps the broccoli go down. You'll be happy because it's loaded with calcium for growing bones.

- 1 cup of broccoli florets
- 1 tablespoon of cheddar cheese

Steam *broccoli for a few minutes until soft, but retaining green color.*

Add *cheddar cheese and let melt for a minute.*

Remove *and serve over rice cakes for a crunchy treat.*

Cheesy broccoli crunch

- 3–4 broccoli or cauliflower florets
- 1 tablespoon of grated cheddar cheese
- 1 teaspoon toasted whole-grain bread crumbs or zwieback

Lightly steam broccoli or cauliflower in a steamer that fits into a saucepan for around 3 minutes.

Add grated cheese at the end.

Top with toasted bread crumbs or zwieback and serve.

Alternatively, you may place the cooked broccoli on a cookie sheet, sprinkle with cheese and zwieback or toasted bread crumbs, and bake at 350°F for 2 minutes or until cheese melts.

Mashed potatoes three ways
Serve these because you know they'll love them. Potatoes are high in fiber and vitamin C.

1. Home-style mashed
- 3 medium-large russet or Yukon gold potatoes, peeled and cut into chunks
- 1/2 tablespoon olive oil or 1/2 tablespoon of organic butter
- 1–2 tablespoons of milk of your choice

Put potatoes into a heavy pot with enough water to cover.

Cook until tender, about 20–25 minutes.

Drain the potatoes and save a little cooking water if not using milk.

Mash together with olive oil or butter and milk.

2. Sweet mashed
- 2 medium-large russet or Yukon gold potatoes, peeled and cut into chunks
- 2 medium-large sweet potatoes, peeled and cut into chunks
- 1 tablespoon olive oil or 1 tablespoon of organic butter
- 1–2 tablespoons of milk or soy milk

Put *the potatoes into a heavy pot with enough water to cover.*

Cook *until tender, about 20–25 minutes.*

Drain *the potatoes and save a little cooking water if not using milk.*

Mash *together with olive oil or butter and milk.*

3. Potatoes, Cheese, 'n Peas
- 3 medium-large russet or Yukon gold potatoes, peeled and cut into chunks
- 1 cup of fresh or frozen peas
- 1/2 tablespoon olive oil or 1/2 tablespoon of organic butter
- 1–2 tablespoons of milk or soy milk
- 1 tablespoon of grated cheddar cheese

Put *potatoes into a heavy pot with enough water to cover.*

Cook *until tender, about 20–25 minutes.*

Cook *peas in a tiny amount of water and drain.*

Drain *the potatoes and save a little cooking water if not using milk.*

Mash *potatoes with olive oil or butter, milk, and cheese.*

Combine *peas at the end.*

Winter warm-up menu ideas
- Chicken soup
- Shepherd's pie
- Golden apple pudding or cinnamon baked apples

Summer cool-down menu ideas
- Smoothies: orange cream, strawberry-nana smoothie …
- Cucumbers

Oven-baked potatoes

• 1 russet or Yukon gold potato or 1 sweet potato

Wash and scrub skin of the potato.

Brush the outside with a little olive oil and a tiny bit of Celtic sea salt. Poke a few holes with a fork.

Bake at 400°F for approximately 50–60 minutes, turning once.

Remove from oven and cool. You may add toppings. Do not let Baby eat the skin.

Toppings: steamed broccoli with or without cheese, yogurt, a little butter

Be creative!

Baked sweeties

• 1 sweet potato, washed

Place on a baking tray with a little water to keep it moist.

Bake at 400°F for approximately 40 minutes or until soft, turning once.

Remove and let cool.

Add a little butter if desired.

Homemade fries

One taste and they'll love them forever. So good they may never make it to the table. High in omega-6 fatty acids.

• 2 or 3 large baking, russet, or Yukon gold potatoes, washed, peeled, and cut into wedges
• water
• 1 tbsp unrefined olive or safflower oil

Preheat *oven to 400°F.*

Bring *water in a saucepan to a boil and add potatoes for 3–4 minutes (to precook).*

Drain *and pat potatoes dry.*

Put *the potatoes on a baking sheet and coat with oil.*

Bake *at 400°F for at least 20 minutes or until they are golden brown.*

Turn *throughout the baking so they do not stick to the pan.*

Sweet potato fries

The other French fry, sweet and delicious!

- 2 sweet potatoes, washed and cut into wedges
- 1 tablespoon of olive oil

Preheat *oven to 400°F.*

Toss *wedges with olive oil.*

Bake *on cookie sheet for at least 25 minutes or until golden brown on the outside and soft in the middle.*

Turn *occasionally while baking.*

GREEN POWER
Green leafy vegetables pack a punch of nutrients: calcium, iron, vitamin A, and chlorophyll.

Sesame spinach

- 1 cup of spinach, washed (You can also use kale)
- 1/2 teaspoon of toasted ground sesame seeds (gomashio) or a tiny sprinkle of sesame oil

Steam spinach in a steamer basket inside a pot for about 1–2 minutes (retaining green color) and top with gomashio or sesame oil.

Creamy spinach

- 1 cup of spinach, washed
- 1/2 teaspoon of tahini

Steam spinach using a steamer basket for about 1–2 minutes (retaining green color). Mix spinach with tahini. Creamy and delicious!

> Spinach is rich in iron, vitamin C, and beta-carotene. Do you remember Popeye and the energy boost that he got from a can of spinach?

Sweet roasties

- 1 large or 2 medium potatoes
- 1 sweet potato
- 1/2 butternut squash
- 1 teaspoon of olive oil

Preheat oven to 350°F.

Wash, peel, and dice vegetables into 1/2-inch cubes.

Sprinkle the oil on the vegetables and toss to coat.

Bake for about 35 minutes, turning vegetables occasionally, until they are golden brown and soft. You may continue to cook on very low heat (250°F) for up to 30 additional minutes to sweeten them.

Vegetable Main Dishes 🌿
Summer vegetable stew

Is your child not eating his vegetables? Hide them in this tasty stew!

- 1 1/4 cups of vegetable stock or water
- 1 tablespoon of olive oil
- 1 large potato or sweet potato, washed, peeled, and cubed
- 1 fresh cob of corn, kernels cut off, or 1 cup of frozen sweet peaches and cream corn
- 1 medium carrot, washed, peeled, and diced
- 1/2 stalk of celery
- 1/4 cup chopped onion

Sauté onion in a medium saucepan with olive oil on low to medium heat.

Add celery and carrots and sauté for 3 minutes until soft.

Add potatoes or sweet potato and corn and pour in stock or water.

Bring to a boil and simmer for about 25 minutes.

Cool for 5 minutes.

Mash a little and serve.

Noodles 'n sauce

- 1/4 medium onion, diced
- 1 medium carrot, diced
- 1/4 medium zucchini, diced
- 1 tablespoon of extra-virgin olive oil
- 3 large ripe tomatoes or 6 plum tomatoes, washed
- 1/4 cup red bell pepper, diced
- 3/4 cup of water

- 1/2 cup of fun pasta shapes, alphabet, stars....
- 1 pinch of herbamare seasoning

Sauce
Sauté *the onion on medium heat in a saucepan for a couple of minutes until soft.*

Add *the zucchini, carrots, and red pepper.*

Cook *for another 4–5 minutes.*

Add *the water and tomatoes; simmer for another 20 minutes.*

Noodles
Cook *the pasta noodles until soft, but not mushy.*

Puree *the tomato and vegetable sauce, leaving a little texture.*

Add *the drained noodles to the sauce and serve.*

You can try different types of vegetables, such as fresh corn kernels or peas. Be creative!

Spaghetti splendor (fourteen to eighteen months)

- 1/4 cup of diced onion
- 1 tablespoon of olive oil
- 4 ounces (1/2 cup) of lean ground beef, turkey, or chicken
- 5 ripe tomatoes
- 1/2 cup of diced zucchini (optional)
- 1/4 teaspoon of herbamare (seasoning)
- 1 cup of water, or vegetable or chicken stock
- 2 ounces (a handful) of whole-wheat spaghetti

Tomato-meat sauce

Heat oil on medium heat in saucepan and sauté onion and zucchini for 2 minutes until soft.

Brown the meat by sautéing it in a dry fry pan.

Add the tomatoes, onion, zucchini, and herbamare and simmer for 20 minutes.

Noodles

Cook the spaghetti until tender with a pinch of sea salt.

Puree the meat mixture with a hand blender, leaving some texture for your toddler.

Chop up the spaghetti into bite-size pieces and add to tomato-meat mixture.

Vegetarian version: Use firm organic tofu instead of meat and crumble it into the sauce.

Theme menu for twelve to eighteen months: Italian

- Minestrone soup
- Noodles 'n sauce
- Spaghetti splendor
- Fruit chunks

Millet patties (fifteen months plus)

So tasty, you'll be nibbling before they reach the table!

- 2 cups cooked millet

- 1 tbsp carrot, shredded
- 1 tbsp chopped onion
- 1 tbsp grated celery
- 1/4 tsp herbamare seasoning
- 1 tsp ground sesame seeds or pumpkin seeds (dry roasted)
- 1/2 tablespoon of olive oil

Combine all ingredients and form into patties.

Sauté patties on medium-low heat in oil until lightly browned. Break into pieces and serve.

Fried brown rice (eighteen months)

- 1/4 cup of onion
- 1 teaspoon of olive oil
- 1 cup cooked brown rice
- 1 egg, beaten
- 1/2 cup of frozen peas, cooked (optional)

Sauté the onion in olive oil in a medium fry pan with a few drops of water for 2–3 minutes until soft.

Add rice and egg and cook on medium-low for 3–5 minutes, stirring until egg is fully cooked.

You may add cooked peas toward the end of cooking.

SOUPS: ONE-POT WONDERS

Soups can be a full meal in one bowl; they are great ways to combine vegetables with protein. Slow-cooked homemade soups take little preparation time and fill your home with mouthwatering aromas and anticipation. Think of soups as a way to relax from your fast-paced lifestyle.

Vegetable soup

- 2 medium carrots
- 2 stalks of celery
- 1/4 finely chopped onion
- 1 tomato, peeled and seeded
- 2 potatoes, washed, peeled, and cubed
- 1 sweet potato, washed, peeled, and cubed
- 1/2 cup zucchini, washed
- 1 cup green beans or peas
- 31/2 cups of vegetable stock or water
- 1/4 teaspoon herbamare

Bring *vegetable stock or water to a boil.*

Add *vegetables.*

Simmer *for 1 hour.*

Puree.

Potato-leek soup

- 5 potatoes, washed, peeled, and diced
- 1 leek
- 4 cups of water or vegetable stock
- 1/2 tbsp vegetable oil

Trim *the root and the top from the leek.*

Wash *thoroughly and chop into small pieces.*

Sauté *leek in a large saucepan in vegetable oil until soft.*

Add *stock or water and potatoes to leeks and boil for about 20 minutes or until very soft.*

Let it cool for about 10 minutes and puree in a blender, food mill, or food processor until smooth.

Beet soup (fourteen months plus)

"Un-beet-able"

- 5 chopped and peeled beets
- 2 tablespoons of chopped onion
- 1/4 cup chopped celery
- 2 chopped carrots
- 1 teaspoon of vegetable oil
- 4 cups of water or vegetable stock

Sauté the onions in oil in a large saucepan until soft.

Add beets, onion, celery, and carrots with water.

Bring to a boil and simmer for about 1 hour.

Puree into smaller chunks.

NOTE: Beets can cause red or pink stools. Do not be alarmed, as this is harmless.

Theme menu for twelve to eighteen months: Vegetarian

- Raw veggies and dip
- Avocado and tahini spread
- Golden pea soup
- Vegetable soup
- Trees 'n cheese
- Millet patties
- Apple-pear crumble

Chicken soup

- 2 organic grain-fed chicken breasts, skinless and boneless
- 2 carrots, chopped
- 1 stalk of celery, chopped
- 1 tbsp chopped onion
- water (enough to boil the amount of chicken used)
- 1 parsnip, if desired

Cut chicken breasts into slices.

Boil water and chicken together, skimming the fat.

Add carrots, celery, onion, and parsnip to the soup.

Simmer for 1 1/2 hours (covered); you may add a boiled potato to thicken if desired.

Puree soup a little in a blender.

You can substitute or add other vegetables such as sweet potato or zucchini. If desired, serve with cooked alphabet noodles or other small pasta.

Best-ever beans 'n barley

- 1 cup of barley
- 2 carrots, chopped
- 1 stalk of celery, chopped
- 1 medium potato, diced
- 1/4 cup of chopped onion
- 1 cup of dried white beans—soaked for 4 hours
- 1 tablespoon of vegetable oil
- 1/4 cup ground organic meat (optional)
- water or vegetable stock (enough to boil the ingredients used)

Soak *beans in water for 4 hours or overnight.*

Sauté *onions in vegetable oil.*

Drain *the white beans and rinse; add to onions with fresh water or vegetable stock.*

Bring *to a boil and cook on low heat for about 1/2 hour.*

Skim *the top.*

Add *vegetables (and ground meat).*

Simmer *for about 1 1/2 hours.*

Puree *a little in a blender or mash and serve.*

Butternut squash soup

- 1 squash, cut into cubes
- 1 teaspoon of chopped onion
- 3 cups of water or vegetable stock
- 1 teaspoon vegetable oil

Sauté *onion in vegetable oil.*

Add *squash and water or vegetable stock.*

Bring *to a boil and simmer for 45 minutes.*

Puree *with a little stock.*

Sweet potato, corn, and kale soup
Our family favorite!

- 5 large sweet potatoes, peeled and chopped into cubes
- 1 cup of corn (fresh or frozen kernels)
- 1/2 cup of chopped kale

- 1 teaspoon of vegetable oil
- 1/2 cup of diced onion
- 3 cups of water
- 1/4 tsp herbamare seasoning

Sauté *the onions in oil until soft.*

Add *water, corn, and sweet potato.*

Bring *to a boil and simmer for about 20 minutes.*

Add *kale.*

Simmer *for another 1/2 hour.*

Puree *a little—you may need to drain some of the water.*

> Toddlers like separate things to pick up, such as pieces of tofu or a noodle, so make sure you include these in your child's diet when he is able to chew.

Mild miso soup

Introduce your baby to a taste from Japan!

Miso paste is very salty, so a little goes a long way. It is very nourishing for your toddler, high in B vitamins and protein, and great for digestion and immunity. There are many types of miso paste; organic mild (mellow) soybean miso or miso with tiny amounts of barley is suggested. When you make the miso broth for your family, you can remove some for your child and make hers separately.

- 2–3 cups of spring water

- 1/2 onion
- 1/4 inch piece of kombu
- tiny piece of wakame, broken up
- 1/2 large carrot, sliced thinly
- 1/4–1/2 teaspoon of miso
- 1/4 cup of soft tofu, cut into cubes
- green onion, chopped for topping

Place *the spring water and kombu into a pot, bring to a boil, and skim.*

Reduce *heat to a simmer and cook for 10 minutes, skim again.*

Remove *kombu—if lots of stuff is still floating on top, you may put the broth through a fine mesh strainer.*

Add *the carrots, onion, and soaked wakame and simmer for another 10–15 minutes until vegetables are soft.*

You may take the vegetables out for a toddler who still likes things pureed and mash by hand in a suribachi, and add back to soup.

Remove *a couple of tablespoons of broth and place in suribachi and add miso paste, stir until dissolved and add this liquid to soup. Add tofu if desired.*

Continue to simmer *for about 3–5 minutes; do not boil because it destroys the vitamins and enzymes in the miso.*

Serve your child just a few teaspoons of mild miso soup a couple of times a week. Once he is older (around twelve to eighteen months) he can work up to eating half a bowl, though the miso should still be mild.

> ## Theme menu for twelve to eighteen months: East Asian
>
> - Miso soup
> - Fried rice
> - Adzuki squash
> - Toasted nori
> - Brown rice balls
> - Amasake

Fresh corn chowder

A summer delight!

- 1 tbsp olive oil
- 1/3 leek, diced
- 1 small potato, peeled and diced
- 1 cup spring water
- 1/3 red pepper (optional for color), diced
- 4 fresh corn cobs (or 3 cups frozen corn)
- 1 stalk of celery, diced
- 1/2 tsp herbamare
- 1 bay leaf (optional)
- 1/2 to 1 cup of milk or soy

Sauté *leek in olive oil on medium heat until soft, about 2 minutes.*

Add *fresh corn cobs (or frozen corn) and leek to water and bring to a boil.*

Add *potato, bay leaf, and herbamare, reduce the heat to low, and simmer for 45 minutes.*

Let it cool. *If corn cobs were used, remove cobs from soup, cut off kernels from cobs, and add kernels back to soup.*

Remove bay leaf.

Leave some chunks, or for a smoother soup puree briefly with a hand blender.

Chicken corn chowder

- 1 corn cob or 1/2 cup frozen whole kernels
- 1/4 onion
- 1/4 cup diced chicken
- 1/2 tablespoon of olive oil
- 1 stalk celery, diced
- 1 small potato, diced
- 1/2 cup vegetable stock or water
- 1/4 cup soy milk (optional)
- Pinch of herbamare seasoning or a pinch of salt or 1/4-inch piece of kombu

Sauté the onion in the oil on medium heat for 2 minutes.

Add the corn, onion, chicken, celery, and potato to stock or water and bring to a boil.

Reduce heat and simmer for 25 minutes.

Cool and remove corn from cob if used.

Puree lightly.

Minestrone soup
A taste of Italy!

- 1/2 onion, diced
- 1 teaspoon of olive oil
- 1 large carrot, peeled and diced

- 1 stalk of celery, diced
- 5 large vine-ripened tomatoes or 10 plum tomatoes, diced
- 2 small potatoes, peeled and diced
- 10 fresh green beans, chopped
- 1/2 cup of cooked macaroni noodles, or shells, pasta stars, or other tiny pasta
- 1/2 teaspoon of herbamare
- 3–4 cups of vegetable stock or water
- pinch of sea salt
- 1/4 cup cooked chickpeas

Sauté *onion with oil in large pot on medium heat for 2–3 minutes until soft.*

Add *carrot and celery; cook for 5 minutes.*

Add *the tomatoes, potatoes, green beans, herbamare, stock, and bring to a boil.*

Reduce *heat and simmer for 15 minutes.*

Add *the chickpeas and pasta stars, cooked shells, or macaroni, and cook for 15 more minutes.*

You can puree a little with a hand blender or mash before serving.

SOUPS AND STOCKS

When your toddler's napping, it's raining, or you just feel like cooking, fill your house with these wonderful aromas. Stocks are simple to make and delicious to enjoy. Homemade stocks are fresh, delicious, and do not contain preservatives, excessive salt, or MSG. Freeze them in little ice cube trays and pop them into freezer bags; they are always ready to use. Recipes using frozen stock cannot be refrozen.

Simple vegetable stock

- 1 medium onion
- 1 large carrot
- 1 stalk of celery
- 1/2 leek
- 5 cups of water
- 1 bouquet garni or some fresh herbs—a few sprigs of (parsley, thyme, oregano)
- 1 bay leaf
- 1 garlic clove (optional)

Wash and chop all the vegetables.

Place all the ingredients in a large stock pot, bring to a boil.

Alternatively, you may sauté the onion and garlic in a small amount of olive oil until soft. Then add the water and the rest of the vegetables.

Reduce the heat and simmer for about 1 1/2 hours. As the stock cooks it will reduce, leaving a flavorful broth.

Turn off heat and let it cool for an hour.

Remove the larger pieces of vegetables with a slotted spoon.

Strain the rest through a sieve or a fine strainer.

Cool and use if needed, or freeze in ice cube trays until set and then place cubes in freezer bags, dating each one.

Chicken stock

- 6 cups of water
- 1 carcass from a roast chicken that has no added salt or seasoning, or 1 1/2 pounds of chicken bones

- 1 leek, diced
- 2 large carrots, peeled and diced
- 1 stalk of celery, ends trimmed, diced
- 1 bay leaf
- 1 sprig of fresh parsley
- 1 sprig of fresh thyme
- 1 large onion

Place water and chicken carcass or bones in a heavy stock pot and bring to a rolling boil.

Skim the fat and lower temperature to a simmer.

Add the vegetables and continue to simmer for 1 1/2 hours until the stock has reduced by at least one-third.

Remove from heat, cool, and place the pot in the fridge overnight.

In the morning, remove any solid fat pieces on top.

Remove the larger vegetables and chicken bones and carefully strain the stock through a fine sieve or strainer, making sure that you catch any small bones.

Freeze unused stock in ice cube containers and when set, place cubes in freezer bags, label and date, and use as needed.

MEAT RECIPES

For vegetarians, you can replace ground chicken, turkey, or beef with firm organic tofu in any recipe.

Beefy spaghetti

- 1 cup of whole-grain spaghetti, cooked

- 1/2 cup of lean ground beef
- 1 tomato, cut up

Sauté *the ground beef in a little water until browned.*

Add *the cooked spaghetti and tomatoes.*

Simmer *for 20 minutes.*

Puree *lightly or mix.*

Asian chicken

- 1 cup of diced chicken
- 1/2 cup cooked brown rice
- 1 carrot, diced
- 1 stalk of celery, diced
- 1 tablespoon of onion, chopped
- 1 teaspoon of vegetable oil
- 1 cup of green peas
- 1/4 teaspoon of tamari (natural soy sauce)
- 2 cups chicken or vegetable stock

Sauté *chicken in saucepan with onion in oil for 5–7 minutes until lightly browned.*

Add *carrot, celery, and stock.*

Simmer *for about 20 minutes.*

Add *brown rice and remove from heat.*

Let stand *for 5 minutes until the stock has been absorbed.*

Puree. *You may need to add extra water or stock to get desired consistency.*

Turkey, sweet potato, and apples

Gobble it up!

- 1 sweet potato, peeled and diced
- 1 apple, royal gala or sweet yellow delicious, peeled, cored, and diced
- 1/2 cup of ground organic turkey
- 1 cup vegetable or chicken stock
- 1 tablespoon of olive or good-quality vegetable oil
- 1 tbsp of chopped onion

Add *olive oil to a saucepan and sauté onion until soft on low-medium heat.*

Add *the ground turkey to the onion and sauté for 3–4 minutes until lighter in color.*

Put in *the rest of the ingredients—sweet potato and apple and vegetable or chicken stock or water—and bring to a boil.*

Cover *and let simmer for 25 minutes.*

Mash *slightly to blend all ingredients, keeping some chunkiness.*

> Chicken and turkey are high in protein, tryptophan (for good moods), B-complex vitamins, and zinc.

Chicken in the garden

- 1/2 cup chopped leek or onion
- 4 ounces (1/2 cup) of skinless and boneless chicken breast, diced, or skinless dark meat

- 1 small carrot
- 1/2 cup of green beans, chopped
- 1/2 cup of fresh or frozen green peas
- 3/4 cup of chicken stock, vegetable stock, or water

Sauté *the leek or onion in oil until soft.*

Add *the chicken and sauté for about 3 minutes.*

Add *the carrot and stock or water, and bring to a boil.*

Simmer *for about 15 minutes, add green beans and peas, and continue to cook for another 10 minutes.*

Let it cool *for about 5 minutes.*

Pour off *some of the liquid and set aside.*

Lightly puree *chicken mixture with some liquid, but leave some texture.*

Shepherd's pie (twelve months plus)
Here's some comfort food the whole family can enjoy!

Filling

- 1/2 chopped onion
- 1 tablespoon of vegetable oil
- 2 cups lean ground turkey, chicken, beef, or tofu cubes for vegetarians
- 1/4 cup chopped tomato
- 1 1/2 cups cooked peas, corn, and carrots (fresh or frozen)

Potato topping

- 5 medium potatoes
- 2 tablespoons water from boiled potatoes

- 2 tablespoons of oil
- 1 egg yolk

Sauté *onions in the vegetable oil on low-medium heat.*

Add *ground meat and brown with tomato until crumbly.*

Boil *potatoes, remove the skin when soft, mash with water from the potatoes, and add oil.*

Add *meat mixture with cooked peas, corn, and carrots.*

Top *with mashed potatoes and brush with egg.*

Bake *at 325°F for 1 hour.*

> Meat is high in protein, iron, zinc, and some B vitamins. Buy it organic and hold the chemicals.

Lamb casserole

- 1 baking potato, peeled and diced
- 1 sweet potato, peeled and diced
- 1 small tomato, diced
- 1/4 small zucchini, diced
- One 3-ounce lamb chop, fat trimmed and cut into cubes
- 1/2 teaspoon of herbamare
- 1/4 cup of chopped onion
- 1/2 cup of water, vegetable stock, or chicken stock

Preheat *oven to 350°F.*

Place *all ingredients into a covered small casserole dish.*

Bake *for 15 minutes.*

Lower *heat and cook for another 45–50 minutes until lamb is soft.*

Blend *ingredients, but leave some chunks.*

Lamb is rich in iron, B vitamins, and zinc, and is a healthier meat choice, because commercial lamb grazes more freely and is fed less chemicals. Choose organic if possible.

"GONE FISHING"

Fish is brain food from the sea! It is high in omega-3 fatty acids, protein, B vitamins, calcium, and selenium, which are essential for a healthy nervous system.

Fish menu ideas for twelve to eighteen months
- Vegetable fish stew
- "My first catch"
- Steamed white fish with mashed potatoes

My first catch

- 1/4 cup fresh deepwater ocean fish such as Pacific halibut or tilapia
- 1 cup butternut squash or other winter squash, peeled and cut into small pieces
- 1/4 inch piece of kombu
- 1/2 cup bok choy or kale, cut into small pieces
- 3/4 cup spring water

Place *the water and kombu into a saucepan.*

Bring to a boil *and skim surface, reduce heat to a simmer.*

Add the fish, squash, and bok choy.

Continue to simmer for around 20 minutes until the fish and vegetables are tender.

Put the ingredients into a suribachi and blend with a tiny bit of the broth, then add back to saucepan, or use a moulix or blender to lightly puree.

A great way to serve this dish is to mash some fish mixture with a small amount of freshly cooked cereal such as millet or brown rice or heated cereal.

Steamed white fish

• One 4-ounce piece of deepwater ocean fish: sole, halibut, or tilapia

Steam fish in a steamer, or steamer basket in pot.

Squeeze a little orange juice on top if desired.

Mash gently and serve.

Baked salmon

• One 4-ounce salmon fillet

Preheat oven to 350°F.

Place the salmon on a broiling pan (with holes, on top of a baking pan with a little water).

Bake for 20 minutes until flaky.

Mash gently and serve. You may squeeze a little lemon on top if your baby likes the taste.

Serve with steamed vegetables such as bok choy, carrots, or broccoli.

Salmon is an oily fish rich in omega-3 fatty acids for the brain and eyes.

Creamy fish couscous

They'll lick the plate clean!

- 1 piece of fresh ocean white fish, tilapia, sole, halibut
- 3 cups water
- 2 cups couscous (whole wheat or regular)
- 1 tablespoon of chopped onion
- 1 diced carrot
- 1 diced celery stalk
- 1/4 cup of grated cheese, cheddar or rice or soy

Boil *water.*

Add *fish, onion, carrots, and celery.*

Simmer *for 20 minutes.*

Add *couscous and remove from heat.*

Add *cheese, mix, and puree lightly or mash in a suribachi.*

Veggie fish stew

- 1/4 small onion or 1/4 leek, diced
- 1 small carrot, peeled and diced
- 1/2 cup of celery, diced
- 1/4–1/2 cup of white fish fillet (skinless), diced and bones removed
- water

Place *all the ingredients into a saucepan and cover them with water.*

Boil *mixture.*

Reduce *heat, cover with lid.*

Simmer *for 20 minutes until fish is soft and cooked and the stock become flavorful.*

__Check__ that there is enough water halfway through cooking, at about 10 minutes.

For an extra creamy stew, add a little milk toward the end of cooking.

Vitamins and Minerals Reference

VITAMINS

Vitamins fall into two different categories: water soluble (B vitamins and vitamin C) and fat soluble (vitamins A, D, E, and K). They are important for the normal growth and development of your baby. They must be obtained from foods (preferably) or supplements because they cannot be created in the body.

VITAMIN	FUNCTION	FOOD SOURCES
A	Promotes growth Enhances immune system Assists in forming healthy bones, gums, and teeth Helps maintain good vision Antioxidant	Carrots, broccoli, squash, pumpkin, cantaloupe, mango, dried apricots, spinach, sweet potato, red peppers, liver, eggs

VITAMIN	FUNCTION	FOOD SOURCES
B Complex	Digestion of carbohydrates, proteins, and fats Healthy nervous system New cell growth Muscular, circulatory system Synthesis of hormones Manufactures antibodies Red blood cell formation	Whole-grain cereals, pastas and breads, tofu, legumes, nuts and seeds, avocadoes, eggs, bananas, dairy, dark-green vegetables, animal products, yeast
Folic Acid	Needed for red blood cell formation, protects against neural tube defects during pregnancy, needed in DNA and RNA synthesis	Squash, lentils, legumes, dark-green vegetables, egg yolks, apricots, romaine lettuce, orange juice, spinach, wheat germ, tofu, liver
B12	For a healthy nervous system and red blood cell and DNA formation	Animal products, poultry, meat, dairy, fish, seafood, eggs, and yeast
C	Fortifies immune system Promotes healthy bones, skin, and teeth	Cantaloupe, papaya, tomatoes, citrus, kiwi, dark-green leafy vegetables, bell peppers, broccoli, sweet potato, squash, berries, peaches, apricots, cherries, plums

VITAMIN	FUNCTION	FOOD SOURCES
D	Enhances calcium and phosphorus absorption for formation of strong bones and teeth	Fish and fish oils, infant formulas, sunlight, fortified dairy products and cereals
E	Antioxidant (protects cell membranes) Anticoagulant	Plant foods; wheat germ; vegetable oils such as safflower, corn, soybean, and olive; nuts and seeds; avocadoes; whole grains; dark-green vegetables
K	Blood clotting May be given to newborns to prevent hemorrhage	Green leafy vegetables, broccoli, fruit, whole grains, eggs

MINERALS

Minerals must also be obtained from our diet. There are two classifications: the macro-minerals and the trace elements. Macro-minerals (such as calcium and phosphorus) are required in large quantities, especially by rapidly growing babies and children, primarily for the formation of strong bones and teeth. Trace elements (such as iron and zinc) are essential for normal cell formation and function. Even though trace elements are needed in small amounts, they are vital for health. The processing and refining of foods frequently causes much of their mineral content to be lost.

MINERAL	FUNCTION	SOURCES
Calcium *(macro)*	Builds and maintains bones and teeth Regulates heartbeat Assists in blood clotting Helps maintain nerve function and muscle growth and contraction	Dairy products, dark-green leafy vegetables, broccoli, sesame seeds, molasses, soybeans, legumes, nuts, almonds, salmon and sardines with bones
Iron *(trace)* Heme iron (animal products) Non-heme (plant foods)	Essential for formation of red blood cells (hemoglobin) Component of enzymes	Heme iron—beef, liver, lamb, poultry, egg yolks Non-heme iron—vegetables, whole grains, iron-fortified grains, blackstrap molasses, seaweed, dried fruit (apricots highly absorbable), legumes, lentils, seeds, green leafy vegetables (not highly absorbable)
Zinc *(trace)*	For protein synthesis and metabolism, growth and repair of cells, digestion	Whole grains, pumpkin and sunflower seeds, nuts, wheat germ, eggs, dairy, red meat, poultry, shellfish

MINERAL	FUNCTION	SOURCES
Magnesium (macro)	For bone mineralization, nerve impulse transmission, muscle contraction, energy metabolism, co-factor for enzymes	Nuts and seeds, whole grains, quinoa, dark-green vegetables, legumes, wheat germ, dairy, soybeans, molasses
Sodium (macro)	Essential in maintaining body's proper fluid balance and acid-base balance, involved in muscle and nerve function	Iodized table salt, processed foods such as cheese, cured meats, canned vegetables and canned food
Potassium (macro)	Helps sodium to maintain water balance, assists with keeping the heart muscles functioning properly	Bananas, avocados, mangoes, molasses, soybeans, legumes, wheat germ, orange juice, apricots, raisins, seeds, nuts, milk, yogurt, sweet potatoes, squash
Chromium (trace)	Helps insulin regulate blood sugar levels, part of glucose tolerance factor, aids in protein metabolism	Whole grains, brewer's yeast, broccoli, turkey (dark), red meat, eggs

MINERAL	FUNCTION	SOURCES
Selenium (trace)	Antioxidant, aids vitamin E in preventing cell damage, strengthens immunity	Nuts (Brazil, walnuts), legumes, dairy, wheat germ, whole grains vegetables, yeast, seafood (tuna)
Iodine (trace)	Essential for proper thyroid function (to produce hormone thyroxine)	Kelp, all seaweed, iodized table salt, vegetables from soil rich in iodine
Fluoride (trace)	For strong bones and teeth; increases absorption of calcium	Fluoridated water and food cooked in it, tea

Whole-Foods Suppliers

Bioforce
www.bioforceusa.com; www.bioforce.ca
(800) 641-7555
A Vogel herbamare spice, natural and herbal remedies, and more

Bob's Red Mill
www.bobsredmill.com
(800) 349-2173
grains, beans, flour blends, cereals, and more

Diamond Organics
www.diamondorganics.com
1-888-ORGANIC
Supplier of a very wide range of fresh organic foods

Flora, Incorporated
www.florahealth.com
(888) 354-8138
Fresh pressed oils, supplements, teas, and more

Grain and Salt Society

www.celtic-seasalt.com

(800)- 867-7258

Unrefined sea salts, organic whole foods in bulk, books, and more

Kushi Institute Store

www.kushiinstitute.org

(413) 645-8744

Maine Coast Sea Vegetables

www.seaveg.com

(207) 565-2907

Organic sea vegetables

Omega Nutrition

www.omegaflo.com

(800) 661-FLAX (3529)

Organic flax oil, gourmet oils, nutritional foods, and more

Rapunzel Pure Organics

www.rapunzel.com

(800) 207-2814

Organic cane juice, organic chocolate, and more

South River Miso Company, Inc.

www.southrivermiso.com

Organic, unpasteurized handmade miso

Spectrum Naturals

www.spectrumorganics.com

Cooking oils, flaxseed oils, and fish oils

Websites for Additional Information

American Academy of Allergy, Asthma, and Immunology
www.aaaai.org

American Academy of Pediatrics
www.aap.org

American Dietetic Association
www.eatright.org

Canadian Pediatric Society
www.cps.ca

Center for Food Safety and Applied Nutrition
www.cfsan.fda.gov

Food Allergy and Anaphylaxis Network
www.foodallergy.org

Gluten Intolerance
www.celiac.com

Health Canada
www.hc-sc.gc.ca

La Leche League (breastfeeding resource)
www.lllusa.org

Mumm's Sprouting Seeds
www.sprouting.com

Organic Consumers Association
www.organicconsumers.org

Organic Trade Association
www.ota.com

"Sproutman" Steve Meyerowitz
www.sproutman.com

The International Sprout Growers Association (ISGA)
www.isga-sprouts.org

Toronto Sprouts
www.torontosprouts.com

United States Department of Agriculture
www.usda.gov

United States Food and Drug Administration (FDA)

www.fda.gov

Vegetarian Resource Group

www.vrg.org

World Health Organization (WHO)

www.who.int

❧ Glossary ❧

Acidophilus A beneficial type of bacteria that, when ingested, helps to replenish the healthy flora in the digestive system.

Adzuki bean A small reddish-brown bean that is frequently used in Japanese cuisine. It is a wonderful healing food for the kidneys.

Amaranth An ancient grain that is high in calcium and magnesium, and is beneficial for the lungs. Amaranth and quinoa are the only two grains that contain complete proteins.

Amasake A drink of Japanese origin that is made from fermented sweet rice. It is prepared in a variety of flavors such as almond.

Arame A thin stranded brown sea vegetable, a member of the kelp family, used frequently in Japanese cuisine.

Ayurveda (or *Ayurvedic*) An East Indian discipline of life and self-healing. "Ayurveda" roughly translates as the "knowledge of life."

Basmati rice A long-grain Indian rice that has an aromatic flavor. "Basmati" means "fragrant" in Sanskrit.

Celiac disease A severe condition of chronic gluten intolerance. People with celiac disease must avoid all grains that contain gluten (wheat, barley, rye, oats); acceptable grains include rice, millet, corn, quinoa.

Colostrum The first milk that mothers produce. It is extremely high in immune-strengthening components, which are passed to the baby during breastfeeding.

Complex carbohydrates Unrefined starches and fiber found in whole grains, fruits, and vegetables; they take longer to digest and provide a more balanced source of energy than simple carbohydrates.

Couscous A small, quick-cooking grain wheat pasta that originates in Morocco.

Gomashio A mixture of toasted, ground sesame seeds and sea salt used as a condiment for rice and vegetables.

Hiziki (Hijiki) A wiry, black-colored sea vegetable usually served as a side dish. It is the seaweed with the highest calcium content.

Kamut An ancient grain that is high in minerals and a great substitute for people sensitive to wheat. It contains more protein and minerals than wheat.

Kombu A seaweed that can be used in soups, stews, and vegetable dishes to add flavor, and to make dishes such as beans more digestible and less gassy.

Kukicha tea (bancha tea) A Japanese tea that is high in calcium and antioxidants, but low in caffeine. It is made from the twigs and stems of the green tea bush.

Lassi A beverage from South East Asia, made with fresh fruit, yogurt, spices, and honey.

Macrobiotic A "whole foods" way of eating that is based on balance and harmony. It is a diet high in complex carbohydrates, emphasizing eating seasonal and local foods.

Miso Fermented soybean paste that is rich in protein. It is made from soybeans, beans, barley, and rice. It is commonly used in soups, stocks, stews, or salad dressings.

Monounsaturated fats A type of "healthy" fat that is found in high concentrations in olive and canola oils, among others. Extensive research indicates that this type of fat offers some protection against cardiovascular disease.

Moulix A hand food mill, especially helpful for pureeing cereals and vegetables.

Mung beans Small, dried green beans (originally from India) that provide lots of energy. Mung dal is the split version of this bean.

Nightshade vegetables A family of foods that includes tomatoes, potatoes, eggplant, and peppers. They contain a substance called solanine, a calcium inhibitor that can interfere with the enzymes in muscles. They have recently been implicated in the aggravation of arthritis.

Nori A seaweed that is formed into thin dry rectangular sheets. Its color varies from greenish-black when toasted (like that used to make sushi) to brownish-black when untoasted.

Omega-3 fatty acids Essential fatty acids that are found in some deep-water fish, plant-based sources such as flaxseed, some nuts, and dark-green leafy vegetables. They are needed for nerves, brain, hormones, and healthy hair and skin.

Omega-6 fatty acids Plant-based oils found in safflower, sunflower, and corn oils. They help with healthy skin, hormone production, and to reduce inflammation.

Phytochemicals Naturally occurring plant chemicals, such as lycopene in tomatoes and beta-carotene in carrots. One of these vegetables can contain thousands of various phytochemicals.

Probiotics Beneficial intestinal flora that can replenish healthy bacteria in the gut that are essential for digestion. They can be taken in capsule or powder form; some yogurts now contain probiotics.

Quinoa (pronounced *keenwa*) A South American grain that is high in protein and contains all the essential amino acids. It is gluten free and may be used in lieu of rice or couscous.

Simple carbohydrates Small molecules of sugar from sources such as white sugar (sucrose), honey, corn syrup, and fruit (fructose). Simple carbs take very little time to digest, and enter the bloodstream quickly, causing sugar highs and lows. They are widely found in processed food. Fruit contains natural simple sugars, but also has fiber so it takes longer to digest.

Spelt A grain closely related to wheat. It is usually well tolerated by people who are allergic to wheat gluten.

Stevia A sweetener that is grown from a small plant in South America. It is extremely sweet, but a healthy sugar alternative if unrefined varieties are used and if it is bought as a green or brown powder, not a white or clear powder.

Suribachi A suribachi is a serrated, ceramic grinding bowl that is used with a wooden pestle (surikogi). It can be used to gently mash or puree baby food. It is very quiet and easy to use and clean. It is commonly used to make gomashio (ground sesame seeds and salt). It can be readily found in Asian stores selling utensils and kitchen equipment.

Tahini A seed butter that is made by grinding white sesame seeds until smooth and creamy. It is rich in calcium.

Tamari A naturally fermented soy sauce that is made from soybeans, wheat, and sea salt. It has no chemicals or preservatives.

Tofu Bean curd that is made from soybeans. It is widely used in Asian cooking in soups and sushi, and in North America in vegetable stir-fries, side dishes, and salad dressings.

Umeboshi plums Pinkish-red plums that are salt-pickled and taste sour and salty.

Vegan A strict vegetarian diet. The vegan diet excludes all animal products including dairy products, eggs, fish, and honey.

Wakame A sweet-tasting sea vegetable that has a thin, long shape. It can be used in soups and vegetable dishes, and is very high in calcium. In

Japan it is used to help purify a mother's blood following childbirth. It is eaten as a soup.

Zwieback A slowly toasted bread that is highly digestible and tasty. It makes an excellent, naturally sweet teething toast for babies.

Recipe Index

Subject Index

enzymes, 169
epinephrine injections, 53
Epi-Pen, 53
essential oils, 3
evening primrose oil, 3

F

fats. *See also* fatty acids
    breastfeeding and, 13
    good vs. bad, 27
    healthy, 2–3, 28, 166
    hydrogenated, 3, 27, 127
    low-fat/nonfat, baby and, 42
    monounsaturated, 27, 247
    polyunsaturated, 3, 27
    saturated, 27, 28
    trans, 27, 28
fatty acids, 28. *See also* omega-3 fatty
    acids; omega-6 fatty acids
    fish and, 2–3
    plant-based, 3, 92, 127
feeding diary/journal, 13
feeding schedules. *See also* food
    introduction charts
        for 9–12 months, 125–126
        first month, 83–85
        first solid foods, 82–85
        snacks and, 155
fertilizers, 101
fiber, 29, 92
    moderation and, 166–167
    sources of, 102, 103, 110, 116,
        169, 184, 195, 199

finger foods, 123–124, 140–142
    choking and, 128
fish, 4. *See also specific types of fish*
    baby's needs, 9–12 months,
        150
    contamination and, 4
    deepwater, 4, 42
    nutritious value of, 228
    oils, 2–3, 150
    recipes, 228–231
flaxseed, 3, 13, 27, 127, 166
flaxseed oil, 3, 13, 127, 166
Flora, Incorporated, 238
fluoride, 36
    function of, 238
    sources of, 173, 238
    supplements, 36
folic acid, 7, 31
    function of, 234
    sources of, 7, 32, 87, 173,
        234
    supplements, 9
food additives. *See* additives
Food Allergy and Anaphylaxis
    Network, 242
food intolerance, 57–59
food introduction charts
    6 months, 71–81
    7–8 months, 96–97
    9–12 months, 129
    12–18+ months, 164
food poisoning, 30, 110
food preparation, 65–69

Lundberg Farms, 45
lycopene, 30

M

mackerel, 27
macrobiotics, x, 247
macro-minerals, 235
magnesium, 8, 92
    cereals and, 87
    chocolate and, 6–7, 174
    function of, 237
    milk absorption and, 159
    sources of, 237
    supplements, 9
Main Coast Sea Vegetables, 240
mangos, 31, 32, 43, 48, 140, 178, 184
maple syrup, 10, 30, 157
margarine, 127
marshmallows, 128
meal planning, 49
mealtime
    mess, 79
    play and, 78–79
    tips for, 161–162
    meat, 4. *See also* poultry
    introducing, 9–12 months, 125, 150
    nutritional value of, 227
    organic, 4, 43, 48, 227
    protein and, 4, 26, 227
    recipes, 12–18+ months, 223–228. *For specific recipes, see Recipe index*
    storage, 49

medications, breastfeeding and, 14
melons, 43, 182
mercury contamination, 4
mess, mealtime, 78–79
Meyerowitz, Steve ("Sproutman"), 170, 242
microwave
    food preparation, 66–67
    PVC and, 43
    uneven heating, 68
milk, 158–159
    allergies, 55
    almond, 3, 173, 180
    baby's needs, 9–12 months, 126
    baby's needs, 12-18+ months, 155
    cholesterol and, 158
    cow, 4, 11, 23, 34, 52, 55, 77, 157, 158, 160, 172–173 4, 11, 158, 160
    digestion, 160
    goat, 4, 11, 158, 173
    lactose intolerance, 58, 158
    low-fat/nonfat, 42, 135, 160
    nut, 179–180
    raw vs. pasteurized, 158
    rice, 168
    seed, 179–180
    soy, 173
    warm vs. cold, 4, 158, 160
"milk babies, 126
millet, 2, 76, 92
    cereals, 87–88

minerals, 33–36, 235. *See also specific minerals*
    breast milk and, 16
    guide to, 236–238
    pregnancy and, 7–9
    sources of, 87–88, 92, 141, 169, 181
    supplements. *See* supplements
    vegetarian diet, 171–173
miso, 169, 176, 217, 247
modern-day vegetarians, 166
molasses, 10
monosodium glutamate (MSG), 41, 221
monounsaturated fats, 27, 247
morning sickness, 5–6
moulix, 65, 66, 247
Mumm's Sprouting Seeds, 242
mung beans, 125, 144, 200, 247

N

navy beans, 144
nectarines, 111
new foods, introducing, 156. *See also* food introduction charts
niacin, 87
nightshade vegetables, 58–59, 101, 157, 247
nitrates, 10, 75
nonfat products, 42, 135, 160
non-heme iron, 236
noodles. *See* pasta
nori, 95–96, 141, 248

nutrient deficiency, 155, 165
    B-complex vitamins, 31
    chromium, 8
    iron, 18, 34, 88, 126, 127, 155, 167
    vegan diet and, 166
    vitamin B12, 11, 31, 167
    vitamin D, 22, 33
    zinc, 35
nutrition
    baby's, foundational, 25–26
    when breastfeeding, 10–11
    organic foods and, 38
    during pregnancy, 1–2
nuts, 3, 4. *See also specific nuts*
    milk, 179–180
    omega-3 fatty acids and, 165, 181
    preroasted, 3
    protein and, 3
    tree nuts, 56, 157, 174
    vegetarian diet and, 165, 172

O

oats, 2, 88, 195
oils. *See also* fats; *specific oils*
    cold-pressed, 2, 3, 127
    fish, 2–3, 150
    healthy, types of, 27
    high-quality, 2
    organic, 127
    poor-quality, 3, 127
    unrefined, 3, 127
olive oil, 2, 3, 27

root vegetables, 101, 107

S

safflower oil, 2, 3, 27
salmon, 3, 4, 13, 27, 150, 159
salmonella, 150
salt, 3, 29–30. *See also* sodium
    baby's needs, 9–12 months, 125, 127
    Celtic, 3, 177
    kidneys and, 41, 127
    sea, 3, 30, 177
    table, 30
sardines, 3, 4, 27, 159
saturated fats, 27, 28
sea salt, 3, 30, 177
sea vegetables, 2, 4, 141
    for baby, 7–8 months, 95–96
    calcium and, 158–159
seasonings. *See* salt; spices
seasons, food and, 44–45
seaweed, 89, 96, 141, 158, 169
seeds, 3, 4, 157, 159
    milks, 179–180
    sprouts and, 169–171
selenium
    function of, 238
    sources of, 165, 199, 238
self-feeding
    at 9–12 months, 123–124
    at 12–18+ months, 155–156
sesame
    oil, 2, 3
    seeds, 3, 125, 177

shellfish, 150
shortening, 127
simple carbohydrates, 26, 248
smoothies, 182
snacks
    for baby, 9–12 months, 125–126
    for baby, 12–18+ months, 153, 154–155, 161–162, 178–179
    calcium-rich, 173
    for pregnancy, 5
    trans fats and, 27
    for traveling, 55
soba, 149
sodium, 10. *See also* salt
    function of, 237
    sources of, 237
solanine, 58, 157
sole, 4, 150
solid foods, 71
    bowel movements and, 81
    feeding schedule, 82–85
    first meal, 76–78
    food amount, 80
    growth, baby, 82
    introducing, 74–76
    mealtime play, 78–79
    nursing and, 81
    readiness, 71–73
soups, 212–223
South River Miso Company, Inc., 240
soy/soybeans, 157, 168–169
    allergies, 57, 144
    milk, 173
    oil, 27

watermelon, 6, 43, 45, 140
weaning, 72–73, 74
website resources, 241–243
wheat, 32, 157
    allergies, 46, 53, 54, 57, 58, 88,
        92, 157
    germ, 7, 33
    sprouts, 169
White, E. B., 25
white potatoes, 157
whole-foods diet. *See also* foods
    benefits of, ix–xi
    breastfeeding and, 10–11
    food suppliers, 239–240
    meal planning, 49
    pregnancy and, 2–5
    overview, ix–xi
whole grains, 2, 45–46, 92. *See also*
    specific whole grains
    bulk bins, 45–46
    enriched vs. fortified, 47
    gluten intolerance, 58
    nutrients in, 87–88
    pasta, 47
    phytonutrients and, 30–31
    preparing, 88–89
    storage, 46
    teething toast, 46–47
    zinc, 172
World Health Organization
    (WHO), 72, 243

Y

yoga, x

yogurt, 135, 137
    antibiotics and, 183
    introducing, 124–125, 160
    lactose intolerance and, 58
    recipes, 136–138. *For specific*
        recipes, see Recipe index
Yutang, Lin, 69

Z

zinc, 35
    deficiency, 35
    function of, 136
    sources of, 35, 87, 92, 103,
        152, 165, 172, 195, 225, 227,
        236
zwieback, 140, 250

ABOUT THE AUTHOR

Jacqueline Rubin has twenty years experience as a nutritionist and educator with university degrees in nutrition, family studies, and education. She has appeared on television and radio and is the founder of Healthy Cheeks, a unique company that specializes in the nutritional needs of infants, children, and expectant mothers.

In developing balanced and insightful programs for your family, Jacqueline also draws on East Asian practices including chi kung, macrobiotics, reflexology, Reiki, and yoga.

Jacqueline lives in Toronto, Canada, with her husband and two active children. *Naturally Healthy First Foods for Baby* is her first widely published book.